CW00549840

Jane
PRIDE AND PREJUDICE

by Andrew Davies

Based on the 1995
TV Adaptation

FOR AMATEUR PRODUCTION ENQUIRIES

UNITED KINGDOM AND WORLD
EXCLUDING NORTH AMERICA
licensing@concordtheatricals.co.uk
020-7054-7298

Each title is subject to availability from Concord Theatricals, depending upon country of performance.

written permission of the publisher. No one shall share this title, or part of this title, to any social media or file hosting websites.

The moral right of Andrew Davies to be identified as author of this work has been asserted in accordance with Section 77 of the Copyright, Designs and Patents Act 1988.

USE OF COPYRIGHTED MUSIC

A licence issued by Concord Theatricals to perform this play does not include permission to use the incidental music specified in this publication. In the United Kingdom: Where the place of performance is already licensed by the PERFORMING RIGHT SOCIETY (PRS) a return of the music used must be made to them. If the place of performance is not so licensed then application should be made to PRS for Music (www.prsformusic.com). A separate and additional licence from PHONOGRAPHIC PERFORMANCE LTD (www.ppluk.com) may be needed whenever commercial recordings are used. Outside the United Kingdom: Please contact the appropriate music licensing authority in your territory for the rights to any incidental music.

USE OF COPYRIGHTED THIRD-PARTY MATERIALS

Licensees are solely responsible for obtaining formal written permission from copyright owners to use copyrighted third-party materials (e.g., artworks, logos) in the performance of this play and are strongly cautioned to do so. If no such permission is obtained by the licensee, then the licensee must use only original materials that the licensee owns and controls. Licensees are solely responsible and liable for clearances of all third-party copyrighted materials, and shall indemnify the copyright owners of the play(s) and their licensing agent, Concord Theatricals Ltd., against any costs, expenses, losses and liabilities arising from the use of such copyrighted third-party materials by licensees.

IMPORTANT BILLING AND CREDIT REQUIREMENTS

If you have obtained performance rights to this title, please refer to your licensing agreement for important billing and credit requirements.

PRIDE AND PREJUDICE was first performed at The Talisman Theatre & Arts Centre, Kenilworth, Warwickshire on Monday 26 June 2023, with the following cast.

CAST

ELIZABETH BENNET	Gwen Davis
JANE BENNET	Joanna Ryan McGough
MARY BENNET	Emily Carleton
LYDIA BENNET	Phoebe Dann
KITTY BENNET	Katie Newman
MR BENNET	Graham Buckingham-Underhill
MRS BENNET	Kathy Buckingham-Underhill
MR DARCY	Chris Bird
GEORGIANA DARCY/	
LADY ANNE DE BOURGH	Clara Saunders
MR BINGLEY	Adam Turner
MISS CAROLINE BINGLEY	Siobhan Twomey
MRS HURST/MRS GARDINER	Judy Wellicome
SIR WILLIAM LUCAS/MR GARDINER	Rob Jones
CHARLOTTE LUCAS	Anna McDonald
MR COLLINS/DANCE PARTNER	Simon Moss
LADY CATHERINE DE BOURGH/	
MRS REYNOLDS	Linda Smith-Blain
GEORGE WICKHAM	Glen Guyver-Fletcher
DENNY/DANCE PARTNER/HARRY	Laurie Weston
MAID	Jane Yates
WORKMAN/BUTLER	Steve Sanday

CREATIVE

Director and Staging – Corrina Jacob

Set Designer – Jeevan Nangla

Production Co-ordinator – Stephen Duckham

Stage Manager – Wendy Elliott

Assistant Stage Manager – Emi Burrows

Rehearsal Prompt – Susi Walker

Properties – Jane Yates

Properties Assistant – Rosalyn Forbes

Wardrobe – Dee Francis, Barbara Port and Margaret Clifton

Lighting – Nigel Elliott

Sound – Colin Thomas

Projections – Dik Thacker

CHARACTERS

THE BENNET SITUATION: They're doomed by primogeniture. Mr Bennet's house and surrounding land must go to the eldest son when he dies – but there is no son! The property will then pass to Mr Bennet's nearest male relative, a young clergyman called Mr Collins.

ELIZABETH BENNET – (Lizzy to her family) Our heroine, 20, very bright, very lively, with a mischievous sense of humour. In the modern parlance, she takes no shit from anyone.

JANE BENNET – 23, her older sister. Beautiful, gentle, affectionate, tends to think well of everyone.

MARY BENNET – 18, serious, bookish without being particularly bright, earnest and humourless.

LYDIA – 15, high-spirited, sexually precocious, one of those girls who 'just wanna have fun'. Thoughtless, but not a bad bone in her body.

KITTY – 17, very much under Lydia's influence. Excitable and easily led.

MR BENNET – late 40s, slightly older than Mrs Bennet, clever and dryly witty. Twenty-two years ago, in his youth, he got Mrs Bennet pregnant and did the decent thing and married her, and has stoically endured the consequences ever since.

MRS BENNET – early 40s, was probably a Lydia in her youth. She still has a romantic heart, but now all her energies are devoted to securing advantageous marriages for her daughters. Mr Bennet is 'landed gentry', Mrs Bennet is from a class below.

MR DARCY – late 20s, is so grand that no one dares to call him by his Christian name. Enormously rich, he owns a grand house (Pemberley) and a large chunk of Derbyshire. Clever, proud, and reserved. But somewhere inside there beats a loving heart.

GEORGIANA DARCY – 17, his much-loved sister. Very much looks up to her older brother.

MR CHARLES BINGLEY – 25, is a rich young gentleman from the North. Warm, friendly, eager to see the good in everyone. He might have a slight Yorkshire or North-Eastern accent.

MISS CAROLINE BINGLEY – 20s, his sister. Snobbish and judgmental, but desperate for Mr Darcy's approval.

MRS LOUISA HURST – late 20s, another sister. Miss Bingley's wing-woman. (Mr Hurst is only interested in drinking, card games, and country sports, so didn't want to be in this stage version.)

SIR WILLIAM LUCAS – 50ish, did very well in trade in Meryton, very proud of his knighthood. Good-natured, a bit pompous.

CHARLOTTE LUCAS – early 20s, his daughter. A close friend of Elizabeth's, she has a ruthlessly practical approach to life.

MR COLLINS – 30ish, a rather dim-witted clergyman who has an unjustifiably high opinion of himself. Greatly in awe of Lady Catherine, to whom he owes his living.

LADY CATHERINE DE BOURGH – 50s, a wealthy aristocratic widow, aunt to Mr Darcy. Autocratic, unpleasant and fairly stupid.

LADY ANNE DE BOURGH – her daughter, early 20s, pale and sickly, she suffers from various unspecified health problems. Never speaks in this version.

GEORGE WICKHAM – late 20s, a personable young officer. Childhood friend (and now enemy) of Mr Darcy. We need to think he's going to be the hero when we meet him, he's so charming.

DENNY – 20ish, another officer.

MR GARDINER – late 40s, Mrs Bennet's brother. Kind, sensible and practical.

MRS GARDINER – 30s, affectionate, aunt to Elizabeth.

MRS REYNOLDS – 60s, housekeeper at Pemberley.

HANNAH or **HARRY** – late teens, servant at the Lambton inn.

MAID – servant to all locations as required.

BUTLER or **DANCERS** – extras as desired.

SETTING

The action takes place over at least a year at several locations across England. Georgian England.

TIME

At the end of the 1700s during the time that
Jane Austen was alive (1775–1817).

NOTES ON SCRIPT

MUSIC AND SOUND EFFECTS: Link music between scenes and other music and sound effects. A licence to produce *Pride and Prejudice* does not include a performance licence for any third-party or copyrighted music. Licensees should create an original composition or use music in the public domain. For further information, please see the Music and Third-Party Materials Use Note on page iii. Also see list of suggested music at the back of the script.

PORTRAITS: The portraits mentioned are not a requirement of the set design.

PROJECTIONS: Various locations were shown as back projections at various points in the script but are not necessary, as the script does identify where the action is taking place.

AUTHOR'S NOTES

I first adapted Jane Austen's *Pride and Prejudice* in 1995 for BBC television. It was received with great acclaim, particularly for the performances of Colin Firth and Jennifer Ehle.

More than a quarter of a century later, I was approached by my local amateur theatre, the Talisman in Kenilworth, asking if I knew of a good stage adaptation of the book. I said I didn't, but I would write one.

This stage version is based on my TV adaptation, even including the famous 'wet shirt' scene, which many people think must be in the book. (It isn't). It needs speedy and flexible staging, and works best with minimal scenery and furniture. It should play in under two hours.

I hope this published version will enable many more enjoyable productions of what is to my mind the best romantic comedy of all time.

Andrew Davies, 2024

SYNOPSIS OF SCENES

ACT ONE

Scene One – Longbourn
Scene Two – A Provincial Assembly Room
Scene Three – Longbourn
Scene Four – Netherfield
Scene Five – Sir William Lucas' House
Scene Six – Longbourn
Scene Seven – Netherfield Exterior
Scene Eight – Netherfield
Scene Nine – Longbourn
Scene Ten – Netherfield and Longbourn
Scene Eleven – Road to Meryton
Scene Twelve – Longbourn
Scene Thirteen – Netherfield
Scene Fourteen – Longbourn
Scene Fifteen – Letters
Scene Sixteen – Hunsford
Scene Seventeen – Rosings
Scene Eighteen – London
Scene Nineteem – Hunsford
Scene Twenty – Rosings
Scene Twenty One – Hunsford

ACT TWO

Scene One – Rosings and Hunsford
Scene Two – Hunsford Exterior
Scene Three – Longbourn
Scene Four – Inn at Lampton
Scene Five – Pemberley Exterior
Scene Six – Inn at Lambton
Scene Seven – Pemberley
Scene Eight – Inn at Lambton
Scene Nine – Longbourn
Scene Ten – A Room in London
Scene Eleven – Longbourn
Scene Twelve – A Room in London
Scene Thirteen – Longbourn

ACT ONE

Scene One – Longbourn – The Bennet's Drawing Room

(Opening music* and lights up as **MARY, JANE, LYDIA, KITTY** *and* **ELIZABETH** *enter in turn, from different directions and address the audience:)*

MARY. *(Is pious and humourless.)* It is a truth...

JANE. *(Is all heart.)* ...universally acknowledged...

LYDIA. ...that a single man... *(The very phrase 'single man' excites her.)*

KITTY. ...in possession of a good fortune...

ELIZABETH. ...*must* be in want of a wife!

> (**ELIZABETH**'s *sense of humour inclines to the satirical.* **MRS BENNET** *marches on left.)*

MRS BENNET. Why, of course he must – and why not one of you?

> *(That sends* **LYDIA** *and* **KITTY** *into fits of giggles.)*

Go away, now girls, I want to talk to your father. Mr Bennet!

---

* A licence to produce *Pride and Prejudice* does not include a performance licence for any third-party or copyrighted recordings. Licensees should create their own.

(**MARY**, **JANE**, **LYDIA**, **KITTY** *and* **ELIZABETH** *go off,* **MR BENNET** *comes on left.*)

MR BENNET. My dear?

MRS BENNET. Have you heard that Netherfield Hall is let?

MR BENNET. I have.

MRS BENNET. To a young man of large fortune from the north of England – a Mr Bingley – a single man of large fortune! What a fine thing for our girls!

MR BENNET. How so?

MRS BENNET. Oh, Mr Bennet! How can you be so tiresome? You must know I am thinking of his marrying one of them.

MR BENNET. Is that his design in settling here?

MRS BENNET. Design! Nonsense! How can you talk so? But it's very likely he *may* fall in love with one of them, and therefore you must visit him, and then you see he can return the visit, and invite the girls to Netherfield, and fall in love with one of them, and marry her!

MR BENNET. But have you not considered, my dear, *you* are as handsome as any of them? Mr Bingley might fall in love with you!

MRS BENNET. Oh, don't talk nonsense! I certainly *have* had my share of beauty... (*And she dwells in it for a moment –*) but now I think only of our daughters – and so should you!

MR BENNET. Perhaps I should, though they have none of them much to recommend them; they are all silly and ignorant like other girls...though Lizzy has something more of quickness than her sisters.

MRS BENNET. Mr Bennet! (*Slaps* **MR BENNET** *on the arm.*) How can you abuse your own children so? You take delight in vexing me! You have no compassion for my nerves!

MR BENNET. My dear, you mistake me. I have every respect for your nerves. They have been my old friends these twenty-odd years. Let me put your mind at rest. I called on Mr Bingley yesterday, and he has engaged himself to bring a party to the next ball in Meryton.

MRS BENNET. Oh, Mr Bennet! You were teasing me all the time! How very good you are!

> (**MRS BENNET** *embraces* **MR BENNET** *fervently.*)

MR BENNET. Yes, yes, very well, very well... *(He makes his escape and exits left.)*

MRS BENNET. Girls! Girls! What an excellent father you have! Wonderful news!

> (**MARY, JANE, LYDIA, KITTY** *and* **ELIZABETH** *reappear, from different directions:* **KITTY** *and* **LYDIA** *together,* **JANE** *and* **ELIZABETH** *together,* **MARY** *on her own with a book.*)

JANE. What is it, Mamma?

MRS BENNET. Mr Bingley, who has *five thousand a year,* has taken Netherfield Hall – and he's bringing a party to the ball at Meryton!

LYDIA. Ooh, Mamma! Will there be officers?

MRS BENNET. How should I know, Lydia. But you should all make sure you look your very best!

> (**MRS BENNET, LYDIA, KITTY** *and* **MARY** *exit left.* **ELIZABETH** *and* **JANE** *move across right with a little music.* **JANE** *at her dressing table, combing her hair,* **ELIZABETH** *standing.*)

ELIZABETH. If I could find a man who loved me and would take me for only fifty pounds a year, I should be very well pleased.

JANE. Yes.

ELIZABETH. But such a man could hardly be sensible, and I could never love a man who was out of his wits!

JANE. *(Thoughtful.)* I think...that a marriage where one partner couldn't love or respect the other...could not be agreeable to either party.

ELIZABETH. As we see every day. *(Brightly.)* But beggars cannot be choosers!

JANE. We are not so *very* poor, Lizzy.

ELIZABETH. With Papa's estate entailed away from the female line, we have very little but our charms to recommend us! One of us at least will have to marry very well indeed! And since you are at least five times as pretty as the rest of us, I fear it'll have to be you!

> *(This causes* **JANE** *to turn to the mirror to check her assets before she turns back anxiously to* **ELIZABETH**.*)*

JANE. But I should like... I do so wish to marry for love.

ELIZABETH. And so you shall, I'm sure. But take care you fall in love with a man of good fortune!

JANE. And what about you?

ELIZABETH. Oh, I'm too difficult to please – I shall end up an old maid!

> *(Lights go down right on* **ELIZABETH** *and* **JANE** *as they freeze.)*

Transition...

(Lights come up on **MR DARCY** *and* **MR BINGLEY** *left.)*

MR DARCY. A *ball*? In a provincial assembly room?

MR BINGLEY. Why ever not, Mr Darcy?

MR DARCY. You don't think the company would be somewhat uncouth?

MR BINGLEY. Not at all – and what if they were? I'm very fond of dancing, and I'm ready to stand up with anyone. Are you refusing to come?

MR DARCY. No, that would be ill-mannered. I will come with you, Bingley, and dance with your sisters. I make no further undertaking than that.

Scene Two – A Provincial Assembly Room in Meryton

(The ball. Country dance music begins.*)

*(**JANE** and **ELIZABETH** cross to join the scene. **MISS BINGLEY**, **MRS HURST** enter right and **MR DARCY** and **MR BINGLEY** join them. **MRS BENNET**, **LYDIA**, **KITTY**, **MARY** all enter together left. **SIR WILLIAM** and **CHARLOTTE LUCAS** enter upstage plus any **DANCERS** or extras for the scene.)*

*(**MR BINGLEY** asks **JANE** to dance and they start the dance with a bow and curtsy. There might be room for six or eight **DANCERS**. **ELIZABETH**, **JANE**, **LYDIA** and **KITTY** or maybe all five sisters, with one or two girls standing in for men. Or other **OFFICERS** available as dance partners.)*

*(**MISS BINGLEY** and **MRS HURST** stand aloof, sneering. The ladies stand out for their elaborate headgear and expensive looking dresses. **MISS BINGLEY** whispers snide comments to **MRS HURST** about the local clodhoppers.)*

*(In the dance, **MR BINGLEY** is making good eye contact with **JANE**, who is blushingly delighted. **MRS BENNET** looking on, beaming, and clapping in time to the music.)*

---

* A licence to produce *Pride and Prejudice* does not include a performance licence for any third-party or copyrighted recordings. Licensees should create their own.

(The dance ends, and **MR BINGLEY** *goes over to* **MR DARCY**. **ELIZABETH** *and* **JANE** *are centre to hear what* **MR DARCY** *says.)*

MR BINGLEY. Come, Mr Darcy, I must have you dance!

MR DARCY. Your sisters are disinclined, and I see nothing else to tempt me here.

MR BINGLEY. I wouldn't be as fastidious as you for a kingdom! The room is full of pretty girls!

MR DARCY. *You* are dancing with the only handsome girl in the room.

MR BINGLEY. Oh, she's the loveliest, sweetest – but look, there's one of her sisters who's not engaged, and she's very pretty, to my eye, and looks very agreeable, too.

(He means **ELIZABETH**, *who is amused by this exchange, as* **MR DARCY** *turns and looks her up and down, and their eyes meet before* **MR DARCY** *turns away again.)*

MR DARCY. She is *tolerable,* but not handsome enough to tempt *me.* You had better return to your partner and enjoy her smiles, for you're wasting your time with me.

MR BINGLEY. Very well! I shall!

(Music starts again. * **MR BINGLEY** *goes and takes* **JANE**'s *hand and draws her aside to chat and to enjoy each other's company.* **ELIZABETH** *and* **MR DARCY** *lock eyes again, briefly, then they both turn their backs and walk away from each other. Everyone exits. Lights down.)*

---

* A licence to produce *Pride and Prejudice* does not include a performance licence for any third-party or copyrighted recordings. Licensees should create their own.

Scene Three – Longbourn

(Lights up, scene change, link music. **MR BENNET** *enters and sits centre with a book.* **MRS BENNET** *is very animated.* **ELIZABETH**, **JANE**, **LYDIA**, **KITTY** *and* **MARY** *stand around* **MR BENNET** *who all enter into scene from left.)*

MRS BENNET. Oh, Mr Bennet, what a time we have had! Jane was so admired, there was nothing like it!

LYDIA. Oh, Lord, I'm so fagged!

KITTY. Lydia and I danced every dance!

LYDIA. And Mary none, ha, ha.

*(**MARY** scowls.)*

MRS BENNET. But Mr Bingley favoured Jane above every other girl – he danced the first two with her, and then the next with Charlotte Lucas, which vexed me greatly, then the next two with Jane again, and then he danced with Lizzy, and then – what do you think?

MR BENNET. Enough of his partners! Would he had sprained his ankle in the first dance!

MRS BENNET. Oh, Mr Bennet! But his sisters, if you had seen them! So elegant and refined! But that man he brought with him, Mr Darcy as he calls himself – proud, horrid, and disobliging! For all he may be the richest man in Derbyshire – do you know, he slighted our Lizzy, and wouldn't stand up with her!

MR BENNET. *(Looking at **ELIZABETH**.)* Slighted my Lizzy, did he?

ELIZABETH. I didn't care for him either, Papa, so it's of little matter.

MRS BENNET. Horrid man. If he asks you next time, I
hope you will refuse him to teach him a lesson.

ELIZABETH. I believe I can safely promise you *never* to
dance with Mr Darcy!

> *(Lights down on them left as they all exit,
> taking chair off with them. We then find
> ourselves in Netherfield right.)*

Scene Four – Netherfield

(Lights up, link music. **MR BINGLEY**, **MR DARCY**, **MISS BINGLEY** *and* **MRS HURST** *enter right.)*

MISS BINGLEY.   *(As she enters.)* And so none of the Hertfordshire ladies could please you, Mr Darcy?

*(***MR DARCY*** *gazing into the middle distance.)*

MRS HURST. Not even the famous Miss Bennets?

*(***MISS BINGLEY*** *and* **MRS HURST** *share a little disparaging laugh and sit.)*

MR BINGLEY. Well, I never met with pleasanter people or prettier girls in my life!

MR DARCY. I saw little beauty and no breeding at all. The, ah, eldest Miss Bennet is very pretty, I grant you.

MR BINGLEY. Admit it, man, she's an angel!

MR DARCY. She smiles too much.

MISS BINGLEY. *(Laughing meanly.)* Oh, Mr Darcy! Too cruel! And now we are invited to a party at Sir William Lucas's, who I understand kept a very good *shop* before he became a gentleman – *must* we go?

MR BINGLEY. Of course we must! It would be very rude not to!

MISS BINGLEY. And no doubt your inamorata Miss Bennet will be there?

MR BINGLEY. I certainly hope so!

MISS BINGLEY. *And* her mother – and *all* her sisters! Shall you be able to bear it, Mr Darcy?

MR DARCY. It seems I must.

(Lights down right with link music.)

Scene Five – Sir William Lucas' Home

> *(Piano and stool set left.* **MARY** *sitting at the piano as the scene opens there is the sound of a piano being played not very well.** *Various characters appear for Sir William Lucas's party.* **MISS BINGLEY, MRS HURST, MR DARCY** *and* **MR BINGLEY** *all move into scene from right.* **LYDIA, KITTY, JANE, ELIZABETH, MARY, MRS BENNET** *enter left,* **CHARLOTTE** *and* **SIR WILLIAM** *enter left and cross to* **MR DARCY, MR BINGLEY, MISS BINGLEY** *and* **MRS HURST.** *Any extras or dancers join the scene.)*

SIR WILLIAM. Mr Bingley, Mr Darcy, Miss Bingley, Mrs Hurst, you are very welcome, it is very good of you to grace our modest gathering!

> *(***MISS BINGLEY** *and* **MRS HURST** *looking snooty as before, ditto* **MR DARCY, MR BINGLEY** *is looking eagerly about for* **JANE** *– and there she is, and he goes to greet her. Both very pleased to see each other.* **MR DARCY** *observes them sardonically.* **LYDIA** *and* **KITTY** *are looking frisky, as* **MARY** *continues to play her sombre chords.)*

LYDIA. *(Standing behind* **MARY** *at the piano.)* Oh, Mary! Stop playing that gloomy stuff, play something jolly, we want to dance!

> *(***MARY** *sighs.)*

MRS BENNET. Oh, play us a jig, Mary, no one wants your concertos here!

---

* A licence to produce *Pride and Prejudice* does not include a performance licence for any third-party or copyrighted recordings. Licensees should create their own.

MARY. *(Scowling.)* Very well.

> *(And she does.* **LYDIA** *and* **KITTY** *grab a couple of young* **OFFICERS/DANCERS** *and start dancing, So does* **JANE** *and* **MR BINGLEY**. **SIR WILLIAM** *and* **MRS BENNET** *look on with pleasure, the Mr Darcy party look aloof.* **CHARLOTTE LUCAS** *approaches* **ELIZABETH** *and moves downstage.* **MR DARCY** *is looking across at* **ELIZABETH** *from afar.)*

CHARLOTTE. Elizabeth!

ELIZABETH. Charlotte!

CHARLOTTE. I see Mr Bingley continues his attentions to Jane.

ELIZABETH. I think if it goes on as it has been, she is in a fair way to be very much in love with him!

CHARLOTTE. Then she should leave him in no doubt of her feelings, if she means to secure him!

ELIZABETH. Secure him?

CHARLOTTE. Yes, of course, she must do that as soon as she can.

ELIZABETH. Before she is sure of his character? Before she is sure even of her own feelings?

CHARLOTTE. Yes, of course! Happiness in marriage is always a matter of chance, you know! It's best if she knows nothing of his defects in advance – once they are married she will find out all too soon! She should encourage him as much as she can – he will get very little encouragement from his sisters I think.

ELIZABETH. Or his friend.

CHARLOTTE. Mr Darcy looks at *you* a great deal.

ELIZABETH. I cannot think why – unless he means to frighten me with his contempt.

*(**SIR WILLIAM** accosts **MR DARCY** right.)*

SIR WILLIAM. What a charming activity this is for young people, sir! I consider dancing to be one of the refinements of every polished society!

MR DARCY. Yes, and every *un*polished one.

SIR WILLIAM. Sir?

MR DARCY. Every savage can dance.

SIR WILLIAM. *(Baffled.)* What? Oh! Yes! Ha ha! Very witty, sir! Excellent!

> *(**SIR WILLIAM** is a bit taken aback, but perseveres. Dance ends and they all bow and curtsy. **JANE** crosses to meet up with **ELIZABETH**.)*

Mr Darcy, allow me to present this young lady to you. You cannot refuse, when there is so much beauty before you!

MR DARCY. *(Polite but distant.)* Would you do me the honour, Miss Bennet?

ELIZABETH. Thank you – but I beg you would excuse me.

> *(She walks away with **JANE**. **MR DARCY** looks after her.)*

SIR WILLIAM. Well, well – what's to be done?

> *(**SIR WILLIAM** goes over to talk to **MRS BENNET** and **CHARLOTTE**. **MISS BINGLEY** goes closer to **MR DARCY**.)*

MISS BINGLEY. I think I can guess your thoughts at this moment.

MR DARCY. I would imagine not.

MISS BINGLEY. You are thinking how unbearable it would be to spend many evenings in such tedious company.

MR DARCY. No indeed – I was meditating on the pleasure a pair of fine eyes in the face of a pretty woman can bestow.

MISS BINGLEY. And may one ask whose are the eyes that inspired such reflections?

> *(***MISS BINGLEY*** flutters her eyelashes at ***MR DARCY***. He looks directly at ***MISS BINGLEY***.)*

MR DARCY. Miss Elizabeth Bennet.

MISS BINGLEY. Oh! I am all astonishment. *(She strides off right.)*

> *(***MISS BINGLEY***, ***MRS HURST***, ***MR DARCY*** and ***MR BINGLEY*** exit right. ***SIR WILLIAM*** and ***CHARLOTTE*** exit upstage. ***DANCERS*** and ***EXTRAS*** all exit. ***LYDIA***, ***KITTY***, ***MARY*** and ***MRS BENNET*** exit left. Link music while piano is taken off to leave ***JANE*** and ***ELIZABETH*** onstage.)*

Scene Six – Longbourn

*(**MAID** enters with a letter for **JANE**. She opens it as **MRS BENNET** enters left to find out who the letter is from.)*

MRS BENNET. *(Very excited.)* From Netherfield! Well? What does he say?

JANE. It is from *Miss* Bingley.

MRS BENNET. Oh. Oh, well, that is good too. Let me see, Jane! *(She takes the letter from **JANE**.)* "My dear friend!" That's very good! La di da, la di da, la di da..." beg you would dine with Louisa and me today" that's good!

"as the gentlemen are to dine with Colonel Forster and his officers in Meryton." Oh, well. You must go, of course, and make of it what you can.

JANE. May I have the carriage, Mamma?

(We hear clap of thunder and lightning flash.)

MRS BENNET. Certainly not! You must go on horseback, for it looks like rain, and then you will have to stay the night, and Mr Bingley will see you in the morning! Well, hurry up! And tell the boy to saddle up Nellie!

*(**JANE** and **ELIZABETH** exit left. Lights go down and up again. We start to hear rainfall as **MRS BENNET** – looking out the window – joins **MR BENNET** reading in his library right and speaks to him.)*

There you see, Mr Bennet, what a good idea it was of mine to send her on Nellie!

MR BENNET. Were you planning to have her struck by lightning?

MRS BENNET. No, of course not, what a silly idea, why should I want her to be struck by lightning? It was so that she would have to stay the night!

MR BENNET. And why would you desire that outcome, my dear?

MRS BENNET. Oh, Mr Bennet!

*(She's interrupted by **ELIZABETH** running in left.)*

ELIZABETH. A note's just come from Netherfield – Jane is very unwell, confined to bed with a fever!

MRS BENNET. Oh! The poor girl!

MR BENNET. Well, my dear, if she should die, you may take comfort in knowing it was all in pursuit of Mr Bingley, and under your orders.

MRS BENNET. Oh, Mr Bennet! People don't die of little trifling colds!

ELIZABETH. I think I should go and see her, Mamma.

MRS BENNET. And how will you do that when the horses are wanted on the farm?

ELIZABETH. It's only three miles – I'll walk.

MRS BENNET. In all this dirt and mud? You will not be fit to be seen when you get there!

ELIZABETH. I shall be fit to be seen by Jane, which is all I want. And I shall be back by dinner time.

*(**ELIZABETH** exits right first. Lights down with link music as **MR BENNET** and **MRS BENNET** exit right.)*

Scene Seven – Netherfield – Exterior

(Birdsong/countryside sounds. **MR DARCY** *enters left and he is out with his gun.* **MR DARCY** *raises it to fire, then lowers it when* **ELIZABETH** *marches on, a little out of breath and she is liberally splashed with mud. Muddy bottom of coat, dress and shoes.)*

MR DARCY. *(Startled.)* Miss Bennet!

ELIZABETH. Mr Darcy! *(She's embarrassed. He's aroused.)*

I – I am here to see my sister.

MR DARCY. Of course you are.

(Neither moves. They stand there looking at each other till –)

ELIZABETH. Would you be so kind as to take me to her?

MR DARCY. *(Recovering.)* Of course. Follow me. *(And he leads the way exiting right.)*

(Lights down, link music and set two chairs left.)

Scene Eight – Netherfield Hall

(On one side of the stage, right, **JANE** *lies in bed with* **ELIZABETH** *tending to her but not moving too much. On the other side of stage,* **MISS BINGLEY**, **MRS HURST** *enter and we find* **MR BINGLEY** *standing.* **MR DARCY** *is standing looking offstage/out of a window. Lights up left with two chairs and table.)*

MRS HURST. *(As she enters with* **MISS BINGLEY**.*)* Well, we must allow her to be an excellent walker, I suppose. But her appearance this morning! She looked quite wild!

MISS BINGLEY. What does she mean by this scampering about the country? Just because her sister has a cold! Her hair, Louisa!

MRS HURST. Her petticoats! I hope you saw her petticoats, brother! Six inches deep in mud!

MR BINGLEY. I thought she looked uncommonly well.

MISS BINGLEY. *You* observed it, I am sure, Mr Darcy.

MR DARCY. *(Without turning.)* I did.

MISS BINGLEY. I'm inclined to think you wouldn't wish *your* sister to make such an exhibition of herself.

MR DARCY. I would not.

MISS BINGLEY. I am afraid that this may have affected your admiration for her 'fine eyes'!

MR DARCY. *(Now he turns.)* Not at all. They were brightened by the exercise. *(Turns away.)*

(An awkward pause. **MRS HURST** *comes to the rescue.)*

MRS HURST. But Jane Bennet is a sweet girl! It's very sad she should have such an unfortunate family, such low connections!

MISS BINGLEY. Their uncle, she told us, is in trade, and has a shop in Cheapside!

MRS HURST. Perhaps we should visit, when we are next in town!

(**JANE** *and* **ELIZABETH** *laugh at this.*)

MR BINGLEY. They would be just as agreeable to me if they had uncles enough to fill all Cheapside!

(**MR DARCY** *turns back.*)

MR DARCY. But with such connections they can have little chance of marrying well, Mr Bingley. *That* is the material point.

(*There's a touch of anger in his voice, because he also fancies a girl who is beyond the pale. At this point,* **ELIZABETH** *joins them from Jane's bedside.*)

MR BINGLEY. How does your sister do, Miss Bennet? Is she any better?

ELIZABETH. I'm sorry to say she is very unwell.

MR BINGLEY. Let me send for Dr Jones at once. And, of course you must stay the night here.

(**JANE** *and* **ELIZABETH** *roll their eyes.*)

ELIZABETH. Oh – I wouldn't wish to inconvenience you.

MR BINGLEY. Nonsense – I'll send to Longbourn directly for your clothes.

ELIZABETH. Thank you – you are very kind.

(Lights down, link music. **ELIZABETH** *goes back to* **JANE** *in bed.* **MAID** *enters to help* **ELIZABETH** *take off her muddy coat/dress and shoes. Then* **ELIZABETH** *continues to tend to* **JANE** *and freezes.* **MISS BINGLEY**, **MRS HURST** *are seated,* **MR DARCY** *and* **MR BINGLEY** *are standing but freeze during the next scene.)*

Scene Nine – Longbourn

(Lights up on **MR BENNET** *and* **MRS BENNET** *who enter downstage.* **MR BENNET** *enters with a fishing rod.)*

MRS BENNET. What a thoughtful obliging gentleman Mr Bingley is! Sending for Lizzie's dresses! Though it won't do a scrap of good – that Mr Darcy is so disagreeable and nasty that even Lizzie in her prettiest dress couldn't turn his head!

MR BENNET. Then we must thank providence that she is relieved from his attentions.

MRS BENNET. But it is infuriating that a man like that could be rich, handsome, only three miles away, and yet be so disobliging!

MR BENNET. We must bear it as best we can, my dear. Have you seen my box of trout flies?

MRS BENNET. Oh, bother your trout flies! *(And she storms out left.)*

*(***MR BENNET** *exits left once lights down.)*

Scene Ten – Netherfield and Longbourn

(Lights up on **JANE** *sitting up in bed,* **ELIZABETH** *is making herself presentable/ getting dressed.)*

ELIZABETH. There. Shall I disgrace you?

JANE. You look very pretty, as you well know.

ELIZABETH. Oh, Jane, I would much rather stay with you! The Superior Sisters wish me miles away. Only your Mr Bingley shows me any attention.

JANE. He is not *my* Mr Bingley, Lizzie.

ELIZABETH. I think he very soon will be. Well – wish me luck!

(Lights go up on the other side of the stage, where we find **MR BINGLEY** *playing cards with* **MISS BINGLEY**, *and* **MR DARCY** *staring out of the window.* **ELIZABETH** *crosses to stage left with a book in hand.* **MR DARCY** *goes closer to* **ELIZABETH**.*)*

MR DARCY. Miss Bennet, may I enquire after your sister?

ELIZABETH. Thank you, she is much improved.

MR DARCY. I am glad to hear it.

*(***MR DARCY** *retreats to a writing table/slope, and picks up a quill and paper and starts to write.)*

MR BINGLEY. Will you join us in a card game, Miss Bennet?

ELIZABETH. If you will excuse me, I would rather read.

(Raised eyebrows from **MISS BINGLEY** *and* **MRS HURST**.*)*

MISS BINGLEY. Miss Bennet despises cards, I believe.

ELIZABETH. Indeed I do not. But I do love to read.

MISS BINGLEY. And what do *you* do so secretly, Mr Darcy? *(Goes to* **MR DARCY.***)*

MR DARCY. It is no secret. I am writing to my sister.

MISS BINGLEY. Oh! Dear Georgiana! How I long to see her! Is she much grown since the spring? Is she as tall as me?

MR DARCY. She is about Miss Elizabeth Bennet's height, or a little taller.

MISS BINGLEY. And so accomplished! Her performance at the pianoforte is exquisite! Do you play, Miss Bennet?

ELIZABETH. I do, but very ill.

MR BINGLEY. But all young ladies are accomplished!

MR DARCY. I can't think of half a dozen who would satisfy my notion of an accomplished woman.

MISS BINGLEY. Oh, certainly! A truly accomplished woman must possess a certain air in the way she moves and speaks that shows her superiority.

MR DARCY. And more than that – she should have improved her mind by extensive reading.

ELIZABETH. *(Mischievously.)* After all that, I am surprised that you find *any* young ladies accomplished, Mr Darcy!

MISS BINGLEY. Perhaps you have not had the advantage of moving in society enough, Miss Bennet.

ELIZABETH. Yes, I suppose that must be it.

> *(***ELIZABETH*** and* **MR DARCY** *have been intensely engaged in their verbal battle – neither gives a glance in* **MISS BINGLEY***'s direction.* **MISS BINGLEY** *is getting desperate.)*

MISS BINGLEY. Miss Bennet, shall we take a turn around the room?

ELIZABETH. *(Surprised.)* Yes, if you wish.

> (**ELIZABETH** *takes* **MISS BINGLEY**'s *arm, and they take a few steps around the room.)*

MISS BINGLEY. Will you not join us, Mr Darcy?

MR DARCY. That would defeat the object.

MISS BINGLEY. What do you mean, sir? *(To* **ELIZABETH**.*)* What can he mean?

ELIZABETH. I think we'd do well not to enquire.

MISS BINGLEY. No, we insist on knowing your meaning, sir!

MR DARCY. Why, that your figures appear to best advantage when walking, and I may best admire them from my present position.

MISS BINGLEY. Oh, shocking! Abominable! How shall we punish him, Miss Bennet?

ELIZABETH. Nothing so easy: tease him, laugh at him.

MISS BINGLEY. Laugh at Mr Darcy? Impossible. He is a man without fault.

ELIZABETH. A man without fault? *(Her incredulous tone stings* **MR DARCY**.*)*

MR DARCY. Perhaps that is impossible for anyone. But it has been the study of my life to avoid those weaknesses that can expose a strong understanding to ridicule.

ELIZABETH. Such as vanity, perhaps? Or pride?

MR DARCY. Yes, vanity is a weakness indeed. But pride – where there is a real superiority of mind, pride will be always under regulation.

ELIZABETH. Then it is true! Mr Darcy is a man without fault!

(Her tone is mischievous and mocking, and this stings him sharply.)

MR DARCY. I have faults enough, Miss Bennet, but I hope they are not of understanding. My temper I cannot vouch for. It could be called – resentful. My good opinion, once lost, is lost forever.

*(This has all suddenly become uncomfortably intimate. They are both used to easily winning arguments; now they both feel exposed. And **ELIZABETH** finds she can't maintain her usual playful tone. **ELIZABETH** and **MR DARCY** lock eyes during this exchange. **MISS BINGLEY** is put out and is being ignored.)*

ELIZABETH. That is a failing indeed. But I cannot laugh at it.

MR DARCY. I believe everyone has a disposition towards some particular evil.

ELIZABETH. Your defect is a propensity to hate everyone.

MR DARCY. And yours is to wilfully misunderstand them.

*(**ELIZABETH** and **MR DARCY** still can't take their eyes off each other. **MR DARCY** is already half in love with her, and fighting it. **ELIZABETH** enjoys the battle of wits, but her feelings are not engaged, except she's determined to get the better of him. They are interrupted by **MISS BINGLEY**.)*

MISS BINGLEY. Oh! Someone is coming up the drive! Oh! Mrs Bennet, and two of your sisters! How delightful!

*(**MRS BENNET**, **LYDIA** and **KITTY** enter left with capes on. **ELIZABETH** goes to **MRS BENNET** and whispers that **JANE** is still not well.)*

Mrs Bennet! You are very welcome! I trust you don't find Miss Bennet worse than you expected?

MRS BENNET. Indeed I do, sir, she is very ill, and suffers a great deal – I fear we must trespass a little longer on your hospitality!

(**MISS BINGLEY** and **MRS HURST** sigh.)

MR BINGLEY. But of course.

MRS BENNET. You are very kind, sir. Well, you have a sweet room here! I believe you will never want to leave the county, once you have come here!

MR BINGLEY. Indeed, I'd live in the country forever if I had my choice, what about you, Mr Darcy?

(**MR DARCY** is slightly distracted as thinking about the exchange he has just had with **ELIZABETH**.)

MR DARCY. You wouldn't find the society somewhat confined and unvarying?

MRS BENNET. (Taking instant offence.) Indeed, it is not, sir! The country is a vast deal pleasanter than town, sir, whatever you may say about it!

ELIZABETH. Mamma, you mistake Mr Darcy's meaning.

MRS BENNET. He seems to think the country nothing at all!

ELIZABETH. Mamma.

MRS BENNET. Confined? Unvarying! I would have him know we dine with four and twenty families!

(**MISS BINGLEY** and **MRS HURST** are sneering and smirking at **MRS BENNET**. **ELIZABETH** tries to divert her.)

ELIZABETH. Mamma – have you seen Charlotte Lucas since I came away?

MRS BENNET. Yes, she called yesterday with Sir William! What an agreeable man he is! *That* is my idea of good breeding! And those persons who think themselves very important and never open their mouths quite mistake the matter!

> *(All this is directed at* **MR DARCY**, *who bows and moves to stare out of the window.* **ELIZABETH** *is mortified.* **LYDIA**, *who has noticed nothing, comes unwittingly to the rescue with...)*

LYDIA. Mr Bingley, did you not promise to give a ball at Netherfield? It will be a great scandal if you do not!

MR BINGLEY. I shall be very happy to give a ball here as soon as your sister is recovered – and you shall name the day, if you will.

MRS BENNET. *There* now! *That's* what I call gentlemanly behaviour!

> *(Looking daggers at* **MR DARCY**, *who takes no notice.* **ELIZABETH** *wishes the earth would open up.)*

> *(Link music as* **MRS BENNET, LYDIA, KITTY** *exit, taking capes off and then re-enter with* **MARY. ELIZABETH** *goes to* **JANE** *right and they both cross to left to join the rest of family as they enter again at Longbourn.* **MISS BINGLEY, MRS HURST, MR DARCY** *and* **MR BINGLEY** *move to right and freeze as lights go down on them.)*

Transition – Longbourn

(Lights up left once all the **BENNET**s *are in place.)*

MRS BENNET. Well! Here we are! Home again, home again, jiggety jig!

LYDIA. With a ball at Netherfield to look forward to!

ELIZABETH. Oh, Jane, I'm sorry to say it, your Mr Bingley is as excellent as anyone could wish, but I've never been so happy to leave a place in my life!

(Lights down on them as the **BENNET**s *freeze during the next transition.)*

Transition – Netherfield

*(***MISS BINGLEY, MRS HURST, BINGLEY** *and*
MR DARCY *are right. Lights come up on them.)*

MISS BINGLEY. Oh, how pleasant it is to have one's house to oneself again!

*(***MR DARCY** *is staring out of the window.)*

MISS BINGLEY. But I fear Mr Darcy is missing Miss Elizabeth Bennet's pert opinions and fine eyes?

MR DARCY. *(Without turning round.)* Quite the contrary, I assure you.

(Lights fade as **MISS BINGLEY, MRS HURST,**
MR BINGLEY *and* **MR DARCY** *all exit right.)*

Transition – Longbourn

(Lights up left, link music. **MR BENNET** *comes in upstage with a letter and joins the rest of the family.)*

MR BENNET. My dear, I hope you have ordered a good dinner, for we shall be welcoming a guest.

MRS BENNET. Mr Bingley!

LYDIA. Colonel Forster!

KITTY. Mr Daaaarcy!

MR BENNET. None of these. I am expecting my cousin Mr Collins, who may turn you all out of the house as soon as I am dead.

MRS BENNET. Horrid man.

MR BENNET. Let us not judge him too hastily. Listen to this. *(He reads from the letter.)*

"I am, sir, keenly conscious of however unwillingly injuring your amiable daughters, and I am eager to make amends to one of them at least."

KITTY. What does *that* mean?

MR BENNET. I think he means to make a proposal of marriage to one of you.

LYDIA & KITTY. OOOOH!

*(***MARY*** *looks very prim – she would love to be a vicar's wife.)*

ELIZABETH. Without having met any of us? Can he be a sensible man?

MR BENNET. *(With relish.)* Oh, I think not, my dear. I have every expectation of finding him quite the contrary!

Mr Collins, you are very welcome!

(Lights up right as **MR COLLINS** *enters right, smiling a fake smile, bowing several times.)*

MR COLLINS. My dear Mr and Mrs Bennet! And these are your lovely daughters, I presume?

MRS BENNET. Yes, Jane, Lizzy, Mary, Kitty and Lydia.

(Each of them curtsy in turn, and **MR COLLINS** *bows and bestows his horrible smile on each of them.)*

MR COLLINS. I am overwhelmed by the superfluity of charm! My esteemed patroness, the Lady Catherine de Bourgh, has kindly advised me that I should marry as soon as possible – and what more fitting than that I should choose one of these lovely girls?

MRS BENNET. What indeed? For you will find none finer anywhere in the country, I can tell you that!

*(***MARY*** *is thinking "choose me, choose me!"* **ELIZABETH** *and* **JANE** *are thinking the opposite, while* **LYDIA** *and* **KITTY** *have got the giggles at the thought of this pompous fool choosing any of them.* **MR COLLINS** *speaks confidentially to* **MRS BENNET**.*)*

MR COLLINS. I must confess myself particularly drawn to the eldest Miss Bennet?

(Wrong choice!)

MRS BENNET. Oh! Yes! Jane is admired wherever she goes! But *(Stage whisper.)* I think it very likely that she will soon announce her engagement!

MR COLLINS. Ah!

*(***MR COLLINS*** *swivels and turns the full beam of his desire on* **ELIZABETH**.*)*

MRS BENNET. But my younger daughters – in *their* case I know of no prior attachment!

MR COLLINS. I see!

>   (**ELIZABETH** *is trying to avoid returning his rather alarming gaze.*)

JANE.   We were just about to walk into Meryton, Mr Collins. Perhaps you'd care to come with us, if you're not too tired from your journey?

MR COLLINS. Nothing would please me more! Cousin Elizabeth, would you do me the honour of walking with me?

>   (*He offers his arm, and* **ELIZABETH** *forces a smile and takes it. Lights down, link music, as they all walk upstage as the* **MAID** *and* **BUTLER** *enter with their capes to put on.*)

Scene Eleven – The Road to Meryton

(MR COLLINS and ELIZABETH lead the group as they walk into Meryton. Lights up full stage with sound of birdsong/countryside in background. MR COLLINS is rather slow, and keeps patting ELIZABETH's hand to emphasise points.)

MR COLLINS. No one could be more gracious than my patroness Lady Catherine de Bourgh; I have already been invited to dine twice at Rosings.

ELIZABETH. Rosings is very fine, I imagine?

MR COLLINS. You could hardly conceive, cousin. *One hundred and fifty windows!*

ELIZABETH. *(Mocking him.)* You've counted them?

MR COLLINS. In point of fact I have. And the chimneypiece in the drawing room...

LYDIA. Oh, look, there's Denny. Denny! We thought you were still in London!

(DENNY and WICKHAM, two handsome young officers, stroll on right.)

DENNY. Back now, as you see, with our new recruit. Allow me to introduce Mr Gardiner, George Wickham. Miss Bennet, Miss Elizabeth Bennet, Miss Mary Bennet, Miss Kitty Bennet, Miss Lydia Bennet. And –

ELIZABETH. Our cousin Mr Collins.

WICKHAM. I am delighted to meet you all!

LYDIA. *(Flirting with him.)* Do you like dancing, Mr Wickham?

WICKHAM. Very much, and I hope one day to dance with you, Miss Lydia, if fate should allow it.

*(**WICKHAM** returns **LYDIA***'s flirting by being charming.)*

LYDIA. Oh, I'm sure it will!

KITTY. Look Jane! It's Mr Bingley!

*(**MR BINGLEY** comes on with **MR DARCY** left. As soon as **MR DARCY** and **WICKHAM** see each other, their hackles go up. **MR BINGLEY** doesn't notice as all he wants is to see **JANE**.)*

BINGLEY. How fortunate! We were just on our way to Longbourn to enquire after your health, Miss Bennet.

JANE. I am well, as you see. *(She goes to him. They are so happy to be together.)* I hope you will still be able to come and take tea with us at Longbourn.

MR BINGLEY. Wild horses wouldn't prevent me.

*(They don't notice **MR DARCY** and **WICKHAM** who are still giving each other hard stares. **ELIZABETH** notices the stares between the two of them.)*

MR DARCY. Shall we go, Bingley?

MR BINGLEY. Yes, very well – I look forward to seeing you later, then!

*(**MR DARCY** has already left, with a face like thunder. **WICKHAM** moves close to **ELIZABETH**.)*

WICKHAM. Do you know that gentleman?

ELIZABETH. Mr Bingley?

WICKHAM. No, the other.

ELIZABETH. Mr Darcy? We know him as Mr Bingley's friend.

WICKHAM. I have known him all my life. We played together as children.

ELIZABETH. Really? But –

WICKHAM. Yes. You are surprised at the cold manner of our greeting. I am sorry to say that we are no longer friends.

Are you – much acquainted with the gentleman?

ELIZABETH. As much as I ever wish to be. I've spent three days in the same house with him, and I found him very disagreeable.

WICKHAM. He has done me great harm.

> *(It's like they've found a world of their own – the rest go on without* **ELIZABETH**. **LYDIA** *and* **KITTY** *are flirting with* **DENNY**. **MR COLLINS** *is fuming and* **MARY** *is trying to get him to notice her.* **JANE** *is placidly happy on her own.)*

His father, the late Mr Darcy, was one of the best men I have ever known. My father was his steward. Mr Darcy intended me for the church, and it was my dearest wish to enter that profession. But when he died, the son refused to honour his father's promise, and gave the living to someone else. And so, you see, I have had to make my own way in the world.

ELIZABETH. That is quite shocking conduct. He deserves to be publicly exposed.

WICKHAM. One day he will be. But not by me. I don't have a vengeful temperament. And at present, I have every cause for cheer. I have just joined an excellent regiment. I am surrounded by good friends. And I find myself at present in the most delightful society. So you see, I absolutely forbid you to feel sorry for me!

> *(***ELIZABETH** *responds warmly to this.)*

Scene Twelve – Longbourn

(Lights up on **ELIZABETH** *and* **JANE** *at the dressing table right –* **ELIZABETH** *tidying* **JANE***'s hair with a brush/comb.)*

JANE. I cannot believe it, Lizzy. Mr Darcy may be proud and disagreeable, but to behave in such an un-Christian manner! No, I cannot believe it.

ELIZABETH. But why would Mr Wickham invent such a story? If you had heard him – he speaks so frankly and with such feeling! He has suffered, and he bears his suffering cheerfully, with such a manly spirit.

JANE. I think you like Mr Wickham, Lizzy.

ELIZABETH. I do like him. Jane, did you know that Mr Collins's patron, Lady Catherine, is Mr Darcy's aunt? And that her daughter, Lady Anne, is destined to be Mr Darcy's wife?

JANE. No, I did not. *(After a moment.)* Poor Miss Bingley!

ELIZABETH. Mr Wickham spoke of Mr Darcy's sister too – he said he used to know her very well when she was younger, but that recently she has become proud and disdainful like her brother.

JANE. That is sad, if it's the truth.

ELIZABETH. Jane, everything Mr Wickham said rang true!

*(***MRS BENNET*** enters left and calls as if from 'downstairs'.)*

MRS BENNET. Lizzy! Come here this minute! Mr Collins has something to say to you!

ELIZABETH. *(To* **JANE***.)* Oh no. Can't you say I'm out for a walk, or in the bath?

JANE. She knows you're here.

MRS BENNET. *(Annoyed.)* Lizzy! Come down here immediately!

> **(ELIZABETH** *'goes down' reluctantly, to find* **MRS BENNETT. MR COLLINS** *enters with* **MARY** *following, attending* **MR COLLINS** *with dog-like devotion.)*

MR COLLINS. Ah.

MRS BENNET. Come along, Mary! *(She hustles* **MARY** *out. Now* **MR COLLINS** *and* **ELIZABETH** *are alone.)*

MR COLLINS. My dear Miss Elizabeth...

ELIZABETH. Mr Collins?

MR COLLINS. My dear cousin Elizabeth: As soon – *almost* as soon as I entered the house, I settled upon you as the companion of my future life.

ELIZABETH. I beg you would –

MR COLLINS. Please hear me out. My noble patroness was good enough to give me her advice. "Mr Collins" she said, "you must marry. Choose properly", she said. "Choose a gentlewoman, for my sake, and let her be an active, useful sort of person, not brought up too high. Choose such a person, bring her to Hunsford, and I will visit her!" Think of that!

> **(MR COLLINS** *gets into a kneeling position.* **ELIZABETH** *reacts with alarm.)*

And now nothing remains but to assure you in the most animated language of the violence of my affections.

ELIZABETH. Mr Collins, please!

MR COLLINS. To fortune I am perfectly indifferent. I assure you I shall never rebuke you on that score once we are married.

ELIZABETH. You are too hasty, sir. You forget I have made no answer. Let me do so now. I thank you for the honour of your proposal, but it is impossible for me to accept.

MR COLLINS. Ah. (*He laboriously gets up again.*) I am by no means discouraged. I understand it is usual for young ladies to reject the first advances of the man they mean to accept –

(**ELIZABETH** *is getting cross now.*)

ELIZABETH. Mr Collins, I was perfectly serious in my refusal. Please believe me. You could not make me happy, and I am the last woman on earth to make *you* so.

(**MR COLLINS** *is a little put-out.*)

MR COLLINS. My dear Miss Elizabeth, you should consider that given your circumstances, it is quite unlikely that you will be favoured with another proposal.

ELIZABETH. I must bear that as best I can. Excuse me.

(*And* **ELIZABETH** *walks upstage and paces about.* **MR COLLINS** *exits right.* **MR BENNET** *enters left followed closely by* **MRS BENNET** *as she bursts onto the stage.*)

MRS BENNET. Mr Bennet! Mr Bennet!

MR BENNET. What is it, my dear?

MRS BENNET. You must come and make Lizzy marry Mr Collins, for she says she will not have him, and now he is beginning to say he will not have *her!*

MR BENNET. Then what am I to do? It seems a hopeless case.

MRS BENNET. Speak to Lizzy! Tell her you insist on her marrying!

MR BENNET. Lizzy, come here. (**ELIZABETH** *crosses to* **MR BENNET**.)

I understand that Mr Collins has made you an offer of marriage, and your mother insists on your accepting it?

MRS BENNET. Yes, or I will never see her again!

MR BENNET. An unhappy alternative is before you, Lizzy. From this day you must become a stranger to one of your parents. Your mother insists she will never see you again if you *don't* marry Mr Collins...and I will never see you again if you *do*.

MRS BENNET. *(On a wail.)* Oh, Mr Bennet!

> (**ELIZABETH** *kisses her father.* **KITTY** *and* **LYDIA** *come on.*)

KITTY. Mamma! Mamma! You'll never guess what's happened now!

MRS BENNET. What?

LYDIA. Mr Collins has gone and proposed to Charlotte Lucas!

KITTY. And she's *accepted* him!

> (**MRS BENNET** *emits a strangled howl of rage and grief.* **MR BENNET** *and* **MRS BENNET**, **LYDIA**, **KITTY** *all exit left.* **ELIZABETH** *stays to greet* **CHARLOTTE** *as she enters right.*)

ELIZABETH. Charlotte, how could you?

CHARLOTTE. I am not romantic, Lizzy. I never was. Mr Collins is not the most – intelligent of men, but he is of good character and a kindly disposition. He can offer me a comfortable home, and that is all I ask, and more than many women get.

ELIZABETH. I couldn't marry if it were not for love.

CHARLOTTE. *(They hold both hands in friendship.)* Love can grow – or affection, at least. Look at the marriages around you. How many perfectly loving unions do you observe? I think I have done as well as most.

ELIZABETH. Is Mr Collins still with you?

CHARLOTTE. No, he has gone home to tell Lady Catherine the happy news, and to prepare the cottage for me.

ELIZABETH. Oh, Charlotte, I'll miss you!

(They hug.)

CHARLOTTE. Well, I am not gone yet – and as soon as I am settled at Hunsford you must come and visit me.

ELIZABETH. I should like that very much – and to see Rosings, which I have heard so *very* much about!

(They part, and **CHARLOTTE** *exits right, leaving* **ELIZABETH** *looking after her going off.* **MRS BENNET** *comes on waving an invite.* **JANE**, **MARY**, **KITTY** *and* **LYDIA** *enter behind her as she exclaims...)*

MRS BENNET. Girls! Girls! We have all been invited to a ball at Netherfield!

This will be a compliment to you, Jane.

LYDIA. No, to me, because it was I that asked him! I hope he has invited all the officers! Oh, Lord, none of us have anything decent to wear!

ELIZABETH. Then they will have to take us as they find us.

(Lively music. It might be fun to have a sort of mad ballet/movement in which* **MRS BENNET**, **ELIZABETH**, **JANE**, **KITTY**, **LYDIA**, **MARY** *run off and on in various stages*

---

* A licence to produce *Pride and Prejudice* does not include a performance licence for any third-party or copyrighted recordings. Licensees should create their own.

of dress, finally composing themselves into an orderly group with **MR BENNET**, *on one side of the stage. Lights down, scene change with link music. Piano and stool set left.)*

Scene Thirteen – Netherfield Ball

(Lights up full stage. **MR BINGLEY, MR DARCY, MISS BINGLEY** *and* **MRS HURST** *enter right to welcome their guests.* **SIR WILLIAM** *and* **CHARLOTTE, DENNY,** *plus any other extra guests/soldiers are welcomed by the* **BINGLEY**s *with bows and curtsies. Conversation music in the background.**)

MR BINGLEY. Mr and Mrs Bennet! And *all* your daughters! You are very welcome!

(They all curtsy and bow accordingly.)

MISS BINGLEY. Delightful to see you looking so well, Jane – tell me, are you quite recovered?

JANE. Quite, thank you!

(Then turns to **MR BINGLEY** *and he takes her hand –* **MR DARCY** *looking on with some displeasure.)*

MRS HURST. *(To* **ELIZABETH.***)* Still keeping up your country rambles, Miss Bennet?

*(***ELIZABETH** *responds with a 'yes' nod but is distracted as she searches for* **MR WICKHAM.***)*

LYDIA. Oh! I spy officers! Denny! Carter! Yoohoo!

(She's very loud – **MR DARCY** *looks over with apparent contempt and* **MISS BINGLEY** *and* **MRS HURST** *look at each other – how vulgar! But* **LYDIA** *carries on, oblivious.)*

---

* A licence to produce *Pride and Prejudice* does not include a performance licence for any third-party or copyrighted recordings. Licensees should create their own.

I can't see Wickham, Lizzy, will you be very cross if he's not here?

> *(**MR DARCY** picks up on this, too. **DENNY** comes over to **LYDIA**.)*

DENNY. Miss Lydia, Miss Kitty, Miss Elizabeth, Miss Mary. I am instructed to convey Mr Wickham's compliments and his regrets that he'll be unable to attend the ball this evening. Urgent business in town.

LYDIA. Aaowww!

> *(**LYDIA** and **KITTY** move upstage. **MR DARCY** winces. **DENNY** draws **ELIZABETH** aside so others are not able to hear.)*

DENNY. The business I think would not be so urgent, had he not been obliged to avoid a certain gentleman.

> *(He glances in **MR DARCY**'s direction, and **MR DARCY** looks over as if he's picked up every word.)*

ELIZABETH. Thank you.

LYDIA. Come on, Denny!

> *(**LYDIA** and **KITTY** drag **DENNY** off, to have a giggly conversation with him and **CARTER**, the other officer. **CHARLOTTE** comes over to join **ELIZABETH** as she notices her expression of displeasure.)*

CHARLOTTE. You look a little put out, Lizzy.

ELIZABETH. Oh, it's of no consequence – but yes, I just learnt that a gentleman whose company I enjoy has been obliged to stay away, because he has made an enemy of Mr Darcy. And the fault is all on Mr Darcy's side. Really, Charlotte, he is the most disagreeable –

CHARLOTTE. Lizzy!

(She interrupts **ELIZABETH** *because* **MR DARCY** *himself is approaching.* **ELIZABETH** *turns to face* **MR DARCY**.*)*

MR DARCY. Miss Bennet, if you are not otherwise engaged, will you do me the honour of dancing the next with me?

ELIZABETH. *(Flustered.)* I was not – thank you. Yes. *(***MR DARCY** *bows and walks away.* **ELIZABETH** *turns back to* **CHARLOTTE**.*)* Oh, why couldn't I think of an excuse? Hateful man. I promised myself I would never dance with him.

CHARLOTTE. He pays you a great compliment in singling you out, Lizzy. I really think he favours you.

ELIZABETH. I wish he would not.

CHARLOTTE. You would be a fool if you let your fancy for Wickham lead you to slight a man of ten times his consequence!

(The dance music begins. A slow, stately dance, mainly bowing and changing places.* **MR DARCY** *comes and claims* **ELIZABETH***'s hand, and they dance centre, with other couples in the background.)*

ELIZABETH. *(After a few steps.)* I think we must have a little conversation, Mr Darcy. Even though we are both of an unsociable disposition.

MR DARCY. That is a very inaccurate description of your own character; no doubt you were describing mine. Do you go often to Meryton?

ELIZABETH. We do – and when you met us there the other day, we were just forming a new acquaintance.

---

* A licence to produce *Pride and Prejudice* does not include a performance licence for any third-party or copyrighted recordings. Licensees should create their own.

(**MR DARCY** *says nothing at first, then, bitterly...*)

MR DARCY. Mr Wickham is blessed with the happy knack of making new friends. Whether he is able to keep them is less certain.

ELIZABETH. *(Hotly.)* He has certainly lost *your* friendship, and suffered grievously as a result!

(**SIR WILLIAM LUCAS** *butts in at this point. The dance continues but* **SIR WILLIAM** *is not put off as he speaks.*)

SIR WILLIAM. Mr Darcy! Miss Elizabeth! Such superior dancing! You are very well suited as a couple, just like your sister Jane and your friend Mr Bingley! I think we all look forward to a certain desirable event there! (**MR DARCY** *frowns.*) Perhaps *two* desirable events, ha ha!

ELIZABETH. No, indeed!

SIR WILLIAM. But let me not detain you longer. *(And he goes to join* **MR BENNET** *and* **MRS BENNET** *left.)*

MR DARCY. *(After a few steps.)* I have quite forgotten what we were talking about.

ELIZABETH. I don't believe we were talking at all. Let me ask you something. When I was last at Netherfield, you told me that your good opinion, once lost, was lost for ever.

MR DARCY. You remember correctly.

ELIZABETH. Are you sure you never make a mistake in your judgement? You never allow yourself to be blinded by prejudice?

MR DARCY. I hope not.

ELIZABETH. I hope not too.

(The music comes to an end. All **DANCERS** *bow and curtsy.* **JANE** *and* **MR BINGLEY** *stay together chatting.* **MR DARCY** *goes to join* **MRS HURST**. **MISS BINGLEY** *approaches* **ELIZABETH** *centre.)*

MISS BINGLEY. Miss Elizabeth, I hear you are quite delighted with George Wickham! Let me advise you not to believe all his assertions. He has treated Mr Darcy in a most infamous manner. I don't know the particulars, but I do know that Mr Darcy is not in the least to blame. I pity you, Miss Elizabeth, for this discovery of your favourite's guilt – but really, considering his *descent*, one could not expect much better.

ELIZABETH. His guilt and his descent appear by your account to be the same. Nothing you have said convinces me he is in the wrong in any way.

MISS BINGLEY. I beg your pardon. My remarks were kindly meant.

> *(**MISS BINGLEY** goes to join **MRS HURST** and **MR DARCY**, nose in air, and is clearly telling her about her little chat with **ELIZABETH**.)*

Shall we have some music? I have a great desire to hear a song. Caroline? Oh! I see Miss Mary Bennet has anticipated me!

> *(For **MARY** has slid into place at the piano and is already bonking out introductory chords.* And when she starts to sing her voice is loud but not pleasant – people are wincing.)*

---

* A licence to produce *Pride and Prejudice* does not include a performance licence for any third-party or copyrighted music. Licensees should create an original composition or use music in the public domain. For further information, please see the Music and Third-Party Materials Use Note on page iii.

MRS BENNET. Such an accomplished girl – but then all my girls are accomplished!

SIR WILLIAM. I beg your pardon?

MRS BENNET. *(Yelling.)* All my girls are accomplished!

> *(**MISS BINGLEY** is holding her hands to her ears. **MARY** comes to the end of the verse and is about to start the next, when... **MR BENNET** stops her.)*

MR BENNET. ENOUGH! *(She stops dead.)* You have delighted us long enough, Mary. Let the other young ladies have time to exhibit.

> *(**MARY**, mortified, grabs her music and slinks off. **MRS HURST** takes her place and plays with accomplishment. **MRS BENNET** carries on, in the same loud voice.)*

MRS BENNET. Mr Collins wanted our Lizzy, but she wouldn't have him. He wanted Jane first, you know, but Bingley has taken such a fancy to her we expect their engagement to be announced very soon. And that will be good for the younger girls, you see, for it will throw them in the way of other rich men! What a pity that his friend should be so disagreeable, or he would have been quite the catch too!

> *(**BINGLEY** and **JANE** are deep in conversation. **ELIZABETH** is wincing at her mother's loud voice.)*

ELIZABETH. Mamma!

MRS BENNET. What? Who is Mr Darcy, that I should be afraid of him? I am sure we owe *him* no particular civility!

> *(**MR DARCY**, of course, can hear all this, and **ELIZABETH** is mortified.)*

LYDIA. Lord! I'm so fagged!

> (**MISS BINGLEY** *and* **MRS HURST** *look at each*
> *other in disgust.)*

MISS BINGLEY. Really!

> *(Then we go into a flurry of goodbyes,*
> *thank yous good nights, bows and curtsies*
> *from everybody.* **BINGLEY** *emphasises his*
> *intentions to* **JANE.***)*

(To **JANE.***)* And I hope to see you *very soon*!

> *(Everyone exits as lights down, link music.)*

Scene Fourteen – Longbourn

(Scene change, add three chairs around piano. It's a bright morning at Longbourn. All enter left. **MRS BENNET** *[with sewing] and sits,* **ELIZABETH** *[with a book] sits,* **LYDIA** *[with a bonnet and ribbons] stands by piano and* **MARY** *[with a book] sits.* **KITTY** *runs on.)*

KITTY. Mamma! Jane! Netherfield is all shut up! They've all gone away!

MRS BENNET. What? I don't believe it!

*(***JANE*** *enters in tears and obviously upset, holding a letter/note.)*

JANE. I've just received this note from Miss Bingley.

ELIZABETH. Have they really gone away?

JANE. Yes, to London, and they do not expect to return for some time.

ELIZABETH. Nothing from Mr Bingley?

JANE. No – and his sister says that – that – he is very likely to become engaged to Mr Darcy's sister, Georgiana! Lizzy, perhaps he never cared for me at all!

ELIZABETH. I am sure he did and does care for you, Jane. Miss Bingley sees it, and she wants to prevent it. And she thinks that pushing him together with Georgiana will give *her* a better chance of securing Mr Darcy! But Bingley would be a poor sort of man if he submitted to it. You will see him again soon, Jane – I am sure of it.

(Some music to accompany time passing phase of **ELIZABETH, JANE** *and* **MARY** *moving*

around. * **MRS BENNET** *stays in the same chair as* **ELIZABETH, JANE** *and* **MARY** *move around each of the other chairs and piano stool. They move around and freeze to a count of five, move again and freeze, move around again and freeze before finally* **MRS BENNET** *exclaims...)*

MRS BENNET. Three months gone! I do think it very bad of Mr Bingley, I do indeed! He comes into Hertfordshire, he rents a house, he makes our Jane fall in love with him, and then he goes off to London without a word! If he would only let some other wealthy man take over Netherfield, there might be some hope for our girls – but what use is it, standing empty?

*(***MR BENNET*** enters to join the family scene.)*

ELIZABETH. It isn't Mr Bingley's fault, Mamma, he is a sort of prisoner, and his friend Mr Darcy is his jailer. But I am still convinced he will break free one day soon.

JANE. Please, Lizzy, don't give me false hope. It is over. He may live in my memory as – the most amiable man of my acquaintance, but that is all. I have nothing to hope or fear, and nothing, thank God, to reproach him for.

MRS BENNET. And Mr Collins too! What a snake he turned out to be! Just because Lizzy would not have him, he storms off in a pet and captures Charlotte Lucas! When our Mary would be happy to oblige him!

*(***MARY*** bursts into tears. ***MR BENNET*** crosses to* **MARY.***)*

MR BENNET. Come, come, Mary. Come, come, Jane. Next to being married, every girl likes to be crossed in love

---

* A licence to produce *Pride and Prejudice* does not include a performance licence for any third-party or copyrighted recordings. Licensees should create their own.

once or twice. When is your turn to come, Lizzy? Let Wickham be your man. He's as fine a fellow to jilt a girl as any I've seen.

ELIZABETH. Thank you, sir, but a less agreeable man would satisfy me.

MR BENNET. True, but whatever disasters you suffer, you know you have a loving mother who will make the most of them.

MRS BENNET. I don't know what will become of us, I don't, indeed! And I cannot bear the thought of Charlotte Lucas being mistress of this house when you are gone, and we are all turned out and have to live upon the parish!

MR BENNET. Comfort yourself, my dear. Let us hope for better things. Just think: I may outlive you.

(**MRS BENNET** *wails and bursts into tears.*)

MRS BENNET. Oh, Mr Bennet!

(*Lights down and all exit left, except for* **ELIZABETH** *who moves downstage.*)

Scene Fifteen – Letters

(**CHARLOTTE** *enters right. Lights up.*
CHARLOTTE *is found writing a letter to*
ELIZABETH.)

CHARLOTTE. My dear Lizzy, we are now comfortably
settled at Hunsford, and it would give me great pleasure
if you would come and visit us here.

(**MAID** *enters with cape and travel bag for*
ELIZABETH. *The* **MAID** *helps her with her
cape and hands her the travel bag during the
speech.*)

ELIZABETH. (*She speaks her reply.*) Dear Charlotte, I am
happy to accept. I am greatly in need of diversion, for
Jane has gone to stay with our aunt and uncle Gardiner
in London, where it is to be hoped that she might bump
into a certain Mr B. I hope to arrive on Tuesday week.

(**ELIZABETH** *crosses the stage to 'arrive' at
Hunsford.*)

Scene Sixteen – Hunsford

*(**MR COLLINS** enters and **CHARLOTTE** joins him right.)*

MR COLLINS. My dear cousin Elizabeth! What a pleasure it is to welcome you to my humble abode.

*(**MR COLLINS** indicates their small cottage. **CHARLOTTE** takes **ELIZABETH**'s bag and cape. She places them out of the way.)*

ELIZABETH. You are very kind, sir.

CHARLOTTE. So happy to see you, Lizzy.

ELIZABETH. And I you.

MR COLLINS. Do step inside, cousin.

ELIZABETH. Thank you.

(It's quite a small cottage, so we could suggest that by the way they have to squeeze past each other.)

MR COLLINS. A comfortable dwelling, I am sure you will agree, and eminently suitable for a clergyman in my position.

ELIZABETH. Yes, indeed.

MR COLLINS. This staircase, now, is neither too shallow nor too steep.

*(**MR COLLINS** indicates offstage to a 'staircase'.)*

ELIZABETH. It is a very serviceable staircase, sir. One may go up and down quite easily.

MR COLLINS. Exactly! Exactly! And observe this closet here! What do you say to that?

ELIZABETH. It is – I'm sure it's very convenient, sir, for – for storing things?

MR COLLINS. Exactly! Lady Catherine de Bourgh herself suggested that these shelves be fitted here just as you see!

ELIZABETH. A closet with shelves in it: a happy thought indeed.

MR COLLINS. She is kindness itself: no detail is too small as to be beneath her notice.

CHARLOTTE. Yes, she is a very attentive neighbour.

MR COLLINS. We dine at Rosings twice a week! Twice a week! And we are never allowed to walk home. Her Ladyship always orders her carriage for us – one of her carriages, I should say, for she has several!

CHARLOTTE. Perhaps I should show cousin Elizabeth the house, and then we could all walk in the garden.

MR COLLINS. A capital scheme! I shall await you there.

> (**MR COLLINS** *bows and smirks his way out, right.*)

CHARLOTTE. Mr Collins tends the gardens himself, and spends a good part of every day in them.

ELIZABETH. The exercise must be beneficial.

CHARLOTTE. Yes, I encourage him to be out of doors as much as possible. And then he has to walk to Rosings every day.

ELIZABETH. So often? Is that necessary?

CHARLOTTE. No; but I encourage it. And when he is in the house, he is generally in his book room.

ELIZABETH. And you prefer to sit in this parlour?

> (**ELIZABETH** *and* **CHARLOTTE** *sit.*)

CHARLOTTE. Yes. So it often happens that a whole day passes when we have hardly spent five minutes in each other's company.

ELIZABETH. I see.

CHARLOTTE. I find I bear the solitude very well.

ELIZABETH. I understand. But you dine at Rosings twice a week?

CHARLOTTE. We do.

ELIZABETH. And that is – pleasant?

CHARLOTTE. You must judge for yourself – we are invited there this evening!

> *(Lights down, link music. Scene change.* **ELIZABETH** *and* **CHARLOTTE** *cross into next scene.)*

Scene Seventeen – Rosings

(Scene change, link music. Large throne placed centre, with three other chairs, piano and stool left. **ELIZABETH**, **CHARLOTTE** *cross left for Rosings and sit.* **MR COLLINS** *enters into scene and sits.* **LADY CATHERINE** *enters and sits in her throne,* **LADY ANNE** *enters and stands next to the throne. Lights up.* **MR COLLINS** *of course in an ecstasy of obsequiousness.* **LADY ANNE** *says nothing but has a sickly smile.)*

LADY CATHERINE. So, Miss Elizabeth Bennet. *(To* **CHARLOTTE**.*)* Your friend seems quite a pretty genteel sort of girl, Mrs Collins. *(To* **ELIZABETH**.*)* Your father's estate is entailed upon Mr Collins, I understand?

ELIZABETH. It is.

LADY CATHERINE.. Hmm. Do you have brothers and sisters?

ELIZABETH. Yes, ma'am, I am the second of five sisters.

LADY CATHERINE. Are any of the younger ones out?

ELIZABETH. Yes, all of them.

LADY CATHERINE. What? All five out at once? The younger ones out before the elder are married? That is most irregular!

ELIZABETH. Perhaps. But don't you think, Ma'am, it would be very hard on younger sisters not to have their share of society, just because their elders had not the means or inclination to marry early?

> *(***LADY CATHERINE*** looks at* **ELIZABETH** *with surprise at her opinion.)*

LADY CATHERINE. Upon my word, you give your opinion very freely for so young a person! What *is* your age?

ELIZABETH. I am not one and twenty.

(**LADY CATHERINE** *snorts and looks away.*)

LADY CATHERINE. Did I tell you, Mr Collins, that we expect a visit from my nephew in the next day or two?

(**ELIZABETH** *is startled.*)

Lady Anne will be pleased to see him, will you not, Anne?

(**LADY ANNE** *smiles a sickly smile.*)

Yes; Mr Darcy is a *great* favourite here.

(*All stay and freeze.* **ELIZABETH** *crosses downstage and picks up Jane's letter to read or* **MAID** *enters with a letter.*)

Scene Eighteen – In London

*(**JANE** enters right and speaks her letter while
ELIZABETH reads the letter.)*

JANE. My dearest Lizzy, I have been in London now for
twelve weeks, and no one disappointed in Miss Bingley.
When at last she returned my call, she made it evident
that she took no pleasure in seeing me. And when I
asked after her brother, she said he knew I was in town,
but was much engaged at present with Mr Darcy and
his sister. I must conclude, then, that Mr Bingley no
longer cares for me.

*(**JANE** exits right.)*

Scene Nineteen – Hunsford

(**ELIZABETH** *is still reading the letter.*)

ELIZABETH. I refuse to believe it! He has been worked upon by his sister and his friend! That hateful man!

> (**MR COLLINS** *jumps up from the Rosings scene and bursts across stage to* **ELIZABETH**. **CHARLOTTE** *follows trotting behind* **MR COLLINS**.)

MR COLLINS. My dear cousin! Mr Darcy has arrived at Rosings! And we are invited to dine there with him this evening!

ELIZABETH. Oh. Good.

MR COLLINS. Yes, it is good! It is very good news indeed! How very gracious and condescending of Lady Catherine and her nephew! Quite an honour and distinction to be admitted to my lady's intimate family circle!

Scene Twenty – Rosings

(**ELIZABETH**, **MR COLLINS** *and* **CHARLOTTE** *cross back into the Rosings scene and sit.* **LADY CATHERINE** *still on her throne with* **LADY ANNE** *standing.* **MR DARCY** *enters with his hands behind his back, staring out of window.*)

MR COLLINS. (*Fawning.*) So very good of you, Lady Catherine. Believe me, we are very conscious of the distinction you confer on us, you are, indeed, so very gracious...

(**LADY CATHERINE** *nodding along, satisfied. She can handle any amount of this.* **CHARLOTTE** *grinding her teeth.*)

CHARLOTTE. (*Under her breath.*) Oh, stop it, stop it, stop it...

LADY CATHERINE. Mr Darcy, I believe you are a little acquainted with Miss Bennet?

(**MR DARCY** *turns. His manner for once is quite pleasant.*)

MR DARCY. Yes, we met in Hertfordshire. How do your family do, Miss Bennet? Are they well?

ELIZABETH. Yes, I thank you. My eldest sister has been in town these three months. Have you never happened to see her there?

(**ELIZABETH**'s *tone is quite challenging.* **MR DARCY** *seems just a bit embarrassed.*)

MR DARCY. Ah no. I have not had that pleasure.

(**MR DARCY** *turns away to looks out of the window again. Pause.*)

LADY CATHERINE. Shall we have some music? Do you play, Miss Bennet?

ELIZABETH. A little, and not very well.

LADY CATHERINE. You will never improve unless you practise. If *I* had ever learnt, I should have been a great proficient. And so would Lady Anne, if her health had allowed her to apply. Well, let us hear you, Miss Bennet, and see if we prefer your music to your pert opinions.

> (**ELIZABETH** *goes to the piano and plays something simple.* And* **MR DARCY** *crosses to get closer to her to listen!)*

ELIZABETH. Do you mean to frighten me by coming so close, Mr Darcy?

MR DARCY. I am sure you know that was not my intention.

ELIZABETH. Then what *was* your intention?

MR DARCY. To afford myself the pleasure of seeing you and hearing you play.

ELIZABETH. I suppose I can hardly refuse you that. Though I wish you would not observe me so closely. It makes me uncomfortable.

MR DARCY. Then I beg your pardon.

> (**ELIZABETH** *still dislikes him, she's angry with him for his treatment of Wickham and for stepping in the way of Jane's happiness. And she finds him disagreeable, though she likes arguing with him.* **MR DARCY**'s *in love with her, and* **ELIZABETH** *has no idea.)*

---

* A licence to produce *Pride and Prejudice* does not include a performance licence for any third-party or copyrighted music. Licensees should create an original composition or use music in the public domain. For further information, please see the Music and Third-Party Materials Use Note on page iii.

LADY CATHERINE. What are you talking about over there?

(**ELIZABETH** *stops playing.*)

ELIZABETH. Music, ma'am.

LADY CATHERINE. You would play tolerably well, Miss Bennet, if you practised more. You have a goodish notion of fingering, though your taste is not equal to Anne's. Anne would have been a delightful performer, had her health allowed her to learn.

MR COLLINS. Yes, indeed! Delightful, I am sure!

(**LADY ANNE** *smiles her sickly smile.*)

MR DARCY. (*To* **ELIZABETH**.) Will you not continue?

ELIZABETH. If you wish.

(*[Oh!* **ELIZABETH** *thinks, he's coming on to her as if he likes her or something.] And she plays out the scene.* **ELIZABETH** *crosses to stage right. Scene change. Take throne, piano and chairs off.*)

Scene Twenty One – Hunsford

(**ELIZABETH** *is sitting writing a letter to Jane, and speaking it as well.*)

ELIZABETH. Poor Lady Anne is a pale sickly creature, and I feel very sorry for her. Mr Darcy treats her with contemptuous indifference, as he treats everyone. But Lady Catherine is determined to have him as son-in-law as well as nephew, and she is not a woman to be gainsaid. (*Door knock.*) Oh – someone at the door!

(**ELIZABETH** *goes to the door, and in comes* **MR DARCY**.)

Mr Darcy! Mr and Mrs Collins are gone into Hunsford village – will you sit down?

MR DARCY. Thank you. (*He sits, then gets up, then sits again.*) This seems a very comfortable house.

ELIZABETH. It is, yes.

(*A pause.* **MR DARCY** *gets up again, paces about, then bursts out with –*)

MR DARCY. In vain I have struggled. It will not do. My feelings will not be repressed. You must allow me to tell you how ardently I admire and love you.

(**ELIZABETH** *is so astonished she can't think of anything to say.*)

In declaring myself thus, I am aware that I am going against the wishes of my family, my friends, and, I need hardly add, my own better judgement. The relative situation of our families is such that any alliance between us must be regarded as reprehensible. Indeed, as a rational man, I cannot but consider it so myself. But it cannot be helped. Almost from the first moments of our acquaintance, I have come to feel for you a passionate admiration and regard which has overcome every rational scruple. I beg you, most fervently, to relieve my suffering and consent to be my wife.

(**ELIZABETH** *has had time to recover her resentment and her articulacy.*)

ELIZABETH. In such cases as these, I believe it is the custom to express a sense of obligation. But I cannot. I have never desired your good opinion, and you have certainly bestowed it most unwillingly. I am sorry to have caused you any pain, and I hope it will be of short duration.

(*A pause.* **MR DARCY** *is astonished, and angry.*)

MR DARCY. And this is all the reply I am to expect! I wonder why you make so little effort to be civil in rejecting me.

ELIZABETH. And I wonder why you chose to insult me by telling me you liked me against your will, your reason, and your character! Was that not an excuse for incivility, if I *was* uncivil? But I have other provocations. You know I have. Do you think any consideration would tempt me to accept a man who has ruined the happiness of a most beloved sister? Can you deny that you have done it?

MR DARCY. I have no wish to deny that I did everything I could to separate my friend from your sister. Towards *him* I have been kinder than I have towards myself.

ELIZABETH. And this is not the only cause of my dislike. My opinion of you was formed when I heard of your reprehensible conduct towards Mr Wickham.

MR DARCY. You take an eager interest in that gentleman's concerns!

(*They are both angry now.*)

ELIZABETH. So would anyone who knew of his misfortunes!

MR DARCY. *(Contemptuously.)* Oh, yes, his misfortunes have been great indeed!

ELIZABETH. And of your infliction! And yet you treat them with contempt and ridicule!

MR DARCY. So this is your opinion of me. My faults, according to this calculation, are heavy indeed! But perhaps these offences might have been overlooked, if your pride had not been hurt by my honest confession of my scruples concerning your family connections. I am not ashamed of them. Could you expect me to rejoice in the hope of relations, whose condition in life is so decidedly beneath my own?

ELIZABETH. You are mistaken. The mode of your declaration merely spared me any concern I might have felt for you, had you expressed yourself in a more *gentlemanly* manner.

> (**MR DARCY** *is wounded by this. And* **ELIZABETH** *follows up with –*)

Please understand me: there is *no* way you could have proposed that would have tempted me to accept. *(And there's more.)* From the very beginning of our acquaintance, I was struck by your arrogance, conceit, and your selfish disdain for the feelings of others. I had not known you a month before I felt that you were the last man in the world I would wish to marry.

MR DARCY. You have said enough, madam. I perfectly comprehend your feelings, and now I have only to be ashamed of my own. Forgive me for having taken up so much of your time, and accept my best wishes for your health and happiness.

> (**MR DARCY** *bows, and stalks off.* **ELIZABETH** *stands there, trembling for a moment before*

she exits right. Lights down and some dramatic end of act music.)

End of Act One

ACT TWO

Scene One – Rosings and Hunsford

(Dramatic opening Act Two music as lights up. **MR DARCY** and **ELIZABETH** enter on opposite sides of stage. **MR DARCY** on one side of the stage: he has returned from Hunsford in a state. **ELIZABETH** on the other, alone at Hunsford, also in a state.)*

MR DARCY. How could she...? Ungentleman-like? Was I? And all this time she hated me!

ELIZABETH. Hateful man! How dare he speak of my family with such contempt! And to boast of his cruelty to Wickham and to Jane! And then to claim that all the time he was in love with me! Could it be true?

MR DARCY. Well, I have lost her, and forever. That much is clear. I must forget her. *(He takes a few strides up and down, summoning up his willpower.)* But I cannot bear her to be in the world and thinking ill of me! As regards Wickham, at least, I can defend my conduct.

LADY CATHERINE. *(Offstage.)* Mr Darcy! Mr Darcy! Will you not join us?

MR DARCY. *(Angry.)* Later!

---

* A licence to produce *Pride and Prejudice* does not include a performance licence for any third-party or copyrighted recordings. Licensees should create their own.

*(**MR DARCY** sits down and reaches for paper and a quill from desk/writing slope.)*

MR DARCY. "My dear Miss Bennet…"

*(**MR DARCY** stays writing downstage. Lights down left and stay right.)*

ELIZABETH. What am I to do? To stay here, and risk encountering him again…? Unthinkable. Oh, Jane, how I need you now!

*(**MR COLLINS** and **CHARLOTTE** are back from the village. **CHARLOTTE** is carrying a basket.)*

MR COLLINS. Cousin Elizabeth! Here we are! Shall we take tea?

CHARLOTTE. Lizzy, what's the matter? Are you unwell?

ELIZABETH. No – yes – Charlotte, I must go home to Longbourn – today if possible!

CHARLOTTE. What is it? Your parents? Is somebody ill?

ELIZABETH. No. It's not that.

CHARLOTTE. Then what is it? Tell me, pray.

ELIZABETH. *(Deep breath.)* Mr Darcy called, and we… quarrelled.

MR COLLINS. What? Quarrelled with Mr Darcy? How could you, cousin? Lady Catherine will be most displeased when she hears of it, and your intemperate conduct will reflect upon me!

ELIZABETH. I doubt she will ever hear of it, sir.

MR COLLINS. But to offend a man of such consequence!

ELIZABETH. He offended me.

MR COLLINS. *(Furious.)* That is neither here nor there! Mr Darcy is –

CHARLOTTE. My dear!

MR COLLINS. What?

ELIZABETH. If you would excuse me, I will go to my room, I have a headache.

CHARLOTTE. Of course.

> *(***ELIZABETH*** goes off right. Lights down. **MR COLLINS** and **CHARLOTTE** exit right. Lights up on **MR DARCY**: just a candle light would be good. **MR DARCY** is writing his letter and speaking it.)*

MR DARCY. Be not alarmed on receiving this letter. It will contain no repetition of those sentiments which were this evening so disgusting to you. You must pardon the freedom with which I demand your attention, but I must ask for a just hearing.

> *(***MR DARCY*** goes on writing. Sound of an owl and lights change from night to early morning. Sound of early morning bird chorus. **MR DARCY** finishes his letter, stands and starts pacing.)*

Scene Two – Hunsford – Exterior Next Day

(Bright morning light and birdsong. **ELIZABETH** *enters as if she has let her out quietly and is enjoying the fresh morning air.* **ELIZABETH** *comes face-to-face with* **MR DARCY**! **MR DARCY** *is holding his letter.)*

ELIZABETH. Oh! *(She turns away.)*

MR DARCY. Miss Bennet! *(She turns back.)* I have been walking in the grove in the hope of meeting you. Would you do me the honour of reading this letter?

*(***ELIZABETH** *holds out her hand and takes it. Too shocked to speak.)* Thank you.

*(***MR DARCY** *bows and goes downstage left. In a bit of a daze,* **ELIZABETH** *sits down right and opens the letter. Light both separate areas. As she reads it, he speaks the words.)*

"First let me address your accusations concerning Mr Wickham. The facts are these: George Wickham and I were boyhood friends – his father was my father's steward. My father had promised him a living when he became of age. But when the time came he refused the living, saying he had no wish to go into the church. This was no surprise to me, as his life was by then quite dissolute. He asked for three thousand pounds instead, and this he was given. We parted, as I thought, forever. But last summer, our paths crossed again, in a manner that gives me great pain to recall.

My sister Georgiana was persuaded to leave the protection of her school and join Mr Wickham at Ramsgate – she was persuaded to believe herself in love, and to consent to an elopement.

ELIZABETH. Oh!

MR DARCY. She was then but fifteen-years-old.

ELIZABETH. Can this be true?

MR DARCY. Fortunately, I was made aware of the scheme and was able to prevent it before it was too late. Mr Wickham relinquished his object, which was of course my sister's fortune of thirty thousand pounds. A secondary motive must have been a desire to revenge himself on me. Had he succeeded, his revenge would have been complete indeed. I have never revealed these events to anyone, and only do so now in the confidence that you will not say or do anything to harm my sister's reputation. I do not blame you for believing Mr Wickham's account: what reason had you to doubt him? I hope, though, that now you will not judge me quite so harshly.

ELIZABETH. No, indeed. *(She thinks for a moment, then bursts out with –)* But you hurt Jane, and that I will never forgive!

> *(***ELIZABETH*** *stands and collects her cape and travel bag upstage.* **MR COLLINS** *[fussing] and* **CHARLOTTE** *[not fussing] enter right.)*

MR COLLINS. Well, my dear cousin, my dear sister I should say, your trunk is safely stowed! I venture you will have much to tell your mother and father!

ELIZABETH. Yes, indeed.

MR COLLINS. I dare say they will be astonished to hear of the munificence of Lady Catherine's hospitality!

ELIZABETH. They will.

MR COLLINS. And the splendour of Rosings itself!

ELIZABETH. With all its windows.

MR COLLINS. Indeed, indeed, and though the Parsonage can pretend to no such splendour, you can report how comfortable our life is here. You have seen how fortunate an alliance your friend has made, and perhaps you have reflected...well, no matter!

(**CHARLOTTE** *steps forward.*)

CHARLOTTE.   Goodbye, Lizzy. *(They embrace.)* Safe journey!

> (**MR COLLINS** *takes* **CHARLOTTE**'s *arm and they stand there with him patting her hand proprietorially, the perfect couple, as* **ELIZABETH** *exits right. Lights down, link music as* **MR COLLINS** *and* **CHARLOTTE** *exit right.)*

Scene Three – Longbourn

(Scene change, three chairs, piano and stool. Lights up as **ELIZABETH** *enters from right,* **MRS BENNET** *[with sewing] seated,* **JANE** *[with sewing] at piano,* **MARY** *[book] seated,* **KITTY** *and* **LYDIA** *[bonnet and ribbons] by piano, enter from left.* **ELIZABETH** *kisses them all, her mum first.* **MRS BENNET** *talks throughout.)*

MRS BENNET. Here you are, Lizzy, home again, your sister came home yesterday, and I hope you had a better time of it than she did, that Mr Bingley has been a bitter disappointment to us all! So how did you find the Collinses? What sort of place is the Parsonage?

ELIZABETH. *(Sitting next to* **MRS BENNET.***)* Quite small, but very comfortably appointed.

MRS BENNET. And now he will have this house as well when Mr Bennet dies and we are all turned out – who is he to own two houses when we shall have none – my nerves are in shreds for thinking about it! And none of you married yet! And you could have had Collins yourself, and saved us all from the workhouse!

ELIZABETH. I am sorry, Mamma.

MRS BENNET. Well, you were always a contrary girl and fond of your own way. Perhaps some other rich man will come and take Netherfield Hall, for what use is it all shut up?

*(***MR BENNET** *enters upstage.)*

MR BENNET. What, is Lizzy home? Come here, Lizzy. *(***ELIZABETH** *does, and he kisses her.)* I am very glad to see you, Lizzy.

ELIZABETH. And I you.

LYDIA. Look at my new bonnet, Lizzy – should I keep it as it is or pull it apart and remake it?

> (**ELIZABETH** *responds positively to* **LYDIA**. *Lights go down left and* **BENNETS** *all freeze.* **ELIZABETH** *and* **JANE** *cross downstage for next exchange alone. They mime chatting as they cross as one of their intimate scenes. Lights up on them.*)

JANE. He *proposed* to you? I can scarce believe it. Not that anyone's admiring *you* should be astonishing. But he always seemed so cold, so distant...and yet he was in love with you all the time. Poor Mr Darcy.

ELIZABETH. You do not blame me for refusing him?

JANE. Blame you? Oh, no.

ELIZABETH. But you blame me for speaking so warmly of Wickham?

JANE. No – for how could you have guessed at his vicious character? – if indeed he *was* so very bad. But Mr Darcy would surely not have invented a story like that, involving his own sister! Perhaps there has been some terrible mistake.

ELIZABETH. No, Jane, that won't do. I'm afraid there's just enough merit between them to make one goodish sort of man, and for my part, I believe it all belongs to Mr Darcy.

JANE. But it is hard to believe ill of Mr Wickham – there is such an expression of goodness in his countenance!

ELIZABETH. Yes – I'm afraid one of them has all the goodness, and the other all the appearance of it!

JANE. But I am sure, when you first read that letter, you could not laugh about it as you do now.

ELIZABETH. No – it made me very uncomfortable. And I had no Jane to comfort me. Oh, how I wanted you then!

(ELIZABETH and JANE embrace.)

ELIZABETH. There's one point I want your advice on. Should we let people know about Wickham's true character?

JANE. Surely there can be no occasion to expose him so cruelly. What is your own opinion?

ELIZABETH. That we should not tell our friends. Mr Darcy has not authorised me to make it public, particularly as regards his sister. And as for the rest – who would believe it? And Wickham will soon be gone. Father tells me the whole regiment is going to Brighton for the summer.

(LYDIA and KITTY cross downstage and invade ELIZABETH and JANE's privacy.)

LYDIA. Lizzy! Will *you* speak to Papa about us going to Brighton? You know he listens to your advice.

ELIZABETH. You flatter me – but in any case, I wouldn't try to persuade him. I think it's a very good thing the regiment should be removed from Meryton, and our family removed from the regiment.

KITTY. Please, Lizzy!

LYDIA. It's not fair!

(ELIZABETH, JANE, LYDIA, KITTY all join MR and MRS BENNET and MARY left as MRS BENNET exclaims...)

MRS BENNET. Mr Bennet, will you not change your mind? I remember, when I was a girl, I cried for two days together when Colonel Miller's regiment left town – I near broke my heart over it!

MR BENNET. Yet here you are, my dear, and none the worse for it.

LYDIA. Well, I'm sure *my* heart will break!

KITTY. And mine! Why should we not all go for the season?

MRS BENNET. Your father is determined to be cruel.

LYDIA. Mrs Forster says she intends to go sea bathing!

KITTY. *I* should like to go sea bathing!

MRS BENNET. A little sea bathing would set me up forever!

MR BENNET. And yet I am unmoved.

MARY. I have no wish to go sea bathing, Papa. Or go to Brighton at all. I would much rather read a book of sermons.

LYDIA. Oh, pooh to that! You just don't know how to have fun, Mary! Just imagine, a whole camp full of soldiers! Oooh! (*She wiggles with anticipation.*)

MR BENNET. A whole camp full of soldiers and my youngest daughter is the thought that terrifies me. I am going to my library. (*And he goes right then sits reading a book.*)

LYDIA. Aaowwwwwww! I want to go to Brighton!

>(**LYDIA** *exits left and goes to fetch a travel bag and cape.* **ELIZABETH** *goes to* **JANE** *as they cross downstage slightly to be alone.* **MRS BENNET**, **MARY**, **KITTY** *stay onstage.*)

ELIZABETH. You're not happy, Jane. It pains me to see it.

JANE. It's just that I did – I still do – prefer Mr Bingley to any other man I have ever met, and, Lizzy, I did believe that *he* – well, I was mistaken, and there's an end of it. In a little while, all will be well, and we shall be exactly as we were, as if I had never set eyes on him.

*(**LYDIA** rushes in left with cape on and travel bag in hand. **ELIZABETH** and **JANE** turn to **LYDIA** as she shouts their names in excitement.)*

LYDIA. Jane! Lizzy! Mamma! I'm going to Brighton after all!

KITTY. It's not fair! *(Stamps her foot.)*

LYDIA. Mrs Forster has invited me, as her 'Particular Friend', to be her companion in Brighton, and Colonel Forster has taken a house for us!

MRS BENNET. Oh, Lydia! What an honour, to be so singled out!

KITTY. Is it not unfair, Lizzy? Mrs Forster ought to have asked me as well, I have just as much right to go to Brighton, even though I may not be her particular friend!

LYDIA. *(At* **KITTY.***)* Ha! Ha! Ha! Ha!

KITTY. Horrid girl!

LYDIA. Well, I shall get her a present I dare say, though there's no call for her to be in a huff just because Mrs Forster likes me above anyone!

ELIZABETH. Before you crow too much about it, remember Papa has not given you permission, nor is he likely to.

LYDIA. Well he has, so there! Ha, ha! *(She stomps off.)*

*(**ELIZABETH** crosses to **MR BENNET** in his library. Everyone else freezes during the exchange.)*

MR BENNET. I understand your concern, my dear, but Lydia will never be easy till she has exposed herself in some public place – and here is an opportunity for her to do so at very little inconvenience or expense to her family.

ELIZABETH. Papa, I think you cannot be aware of the disadvantage to us all that must arise – has already arisen – from Lydia's wild and uncontrolled behaviour.

MR BENNET. Already arisen? Has she frightened away some of your young men? Take heart. Such squeamish youths are not worth your concern.

ELIZABETH. I was speaking in general, not in particular. But please take this seriously. Our very position as a family is called into question by Lydia's thoughtless behaviour. Forgive me, but I must speak plainly. If she is not checked, she will soon be beyond the reach of amendment! And you know Kitty follows wherever Lydia leads. Don't you see how they will be censured and despised – and involve their sisters in their own disgrace? *(She's worked herself up into quite a moral fury.)*

MR BENNET. Come, Lizzy. Come here. *(He takes her hand.)* Do not make yourself uneasy. Wherever you and Jane go, you will be respected and valued. And you will not appear at any disadvantage for having two – or I may say, *three* very silly sisters. We shall have no peace at Longbourn till Lydia goes to Brighton; Colonel Forster is a sensible man, and Lydia is too poor to be an object of prey to any fortune-hunter.

ELIZABETH. But –

MR BENNET. Leave it now, Lizzy. I believe all will turn out well.

> *(***ELIZABETH** *and* **MR BENNET** *cross left to join rest of family.* **MR WICKHAM** *and possibly* **DENNY** *enter right.)*

MR WICKHAM. I felt I could not leave Hertfordshire without saying goodbye to you all.

LYDIA. *(Flirting.)* You won't be saying goodbye to me, for I am coming to Brighton as well!

> *(***KITTY** *gives her a hard poke.)*

MR WICKHAM. Yes indeed.

MRS BENNET. You will look out for her, won't you, Mr Wickham?

MR WICKHAM. I shall make that my especial care, Mrs Bennet!

LYDIA. Oh, no need to worry about me, I'm Mrs Forster's favourite friend!

KITTY. Horrid girl.

> (**MR WICKHAM** *draws* **ELIZABETH** *aside downstage for a short exchange. Rest of the family mime chat amongst themselves.* **MRS BENNET** *fussing over* **LYDIA**.)

MR WICKHAM. I shall be especially sorry to lose *your* company.

ELIZABETH. We must bear the parting as best we can. I shall be leaving myself soon, to tour Derbyshire with my aunt and uncle.

MR WICKHAM. I heard you were lately a visitor at Rosings.

ELIZABETH. I was.

MR WICKHAM. And did you happen to encounter Mr Darcy there?

ELIZABETH. I did.

WICKHAM. How did you find him?

ELIZABETH. I think he improves on closer acquaintance.

WICKHAM. In his manner? I cannot believe he has changed much in essentials.

ELIZABETH. No; in essentials I think he is very much as he ever was.

> (**ELIZABETH** *looking at* **MR WICKHAM** *challengingly: he doesn't know how to take this.*)

MR WICKHAM. Ah!

ELIZABETH. I think my knowing him better improved my opinion of him.

MR WICKHAM. Ah. You surprise me.

ELIZABETH. No; I don't believe I do.

> (**ELIZABETH** *and* **MR WICKHAM** *lock eyes, challenging. They are interrupted by* **LYDIA** *looking offstage and exclaiming...*)

LYDIA. Oh! Colonel Forster's carriage is here! Goodbye! Goodbye! Goodbye! Goodbye, Mamma!

> (**LYDIA** *and* **MRS BENNET** *embrace.*)

MRS BENNET. Oh, I wish I were going too!

LYDIA. Papa. (**LYDIA** *kisses* **MR BENNET***'s cheek.*)

MR BENNET. Try not to be *too* silly.

LYDIA. Goodbye Jane. *(They hug.)* Goodbye Lizzy! *(They hug.)* Goodbye! Don't miss me too much!

MARY. I for one will not.

KITTY. Nor I.

LYDIA. Goodbye! Goodbye!

> (**LYDIA** *finally runs off right.* **MR WICKHAM** *watches her exit.* **MR WICKHAM** *and* **DENNY** *bow and exit right.* **MRS BENNET** *waving goodbye.* **KITTY** *bursts into tears.* **MR BENNET** *crosses to* **ELIZABETH**.*)

MR BENNET. So we are to lose you as well, Lizzy.

ELIZABETH. Only for a month, Papa.

MR BENNET. I shall bear the loss of you less easily than the loss of your youngest sister. I find I endure Lydia's absence uncommonly cheerfully.

(**KITTY** *looks right offstage and points.*)

KITTY. Mr and Mrs Gardiner are here!

(**MR GARDINER** *and* **MRS GARDINER** *enter right. They are welcomed by* **MR BENNET** *and* **MRS BENNET, KITTY, JANE, ELIZABETH** *and* **MARY**.)

MRS GARDINER. This is so good of you, sister, to take care of our children while we indulge ourselves on a tour of pleasure.

MRS BENNET. Nonsense. It is a delight to have them with us, and Jane has such a winning way with little ones, she will teach them and play with them, and love them, won't you Jane?

JANE. I will.

MR GARDINER. We hoped to take in the Lakes, but my business will only allow sufficient time for Derbyshire – but there are beauties enough there to satisfy anyone – with the wild scenery of Dovedale, the Peaks, and Matlock, and the great estates of Chatsworth and Pemberley.

ELIZABETH. Pemberley?

MRS GARDINER. – I grew up not five miles from Pemberley, in the village of Lambton – we shall stay at the inn there, so that I can revisit all my childhood haunts.

(*Lights down and link music.* **MR BENNET** *and* **MRS BENNET, JANE, KITTY** *and* **MARY** *exit left.* **ELIZABETH, MR GARDINER** *and* **MRS GARDINER** *stroll upstage during lights down.* **ELIZABETH** *and* **MRS GARDINER** *could possibly put capes on with* **MAID** *bringing them onstage.*)

Scene Four – Derbyshire – Inn at Lambton Exterior

(Sound of birdsong for start of exterior scene. **ELIZABETH**, **MR GARDINER** *and* **MRS GARDINER** *turn into scene and cross downstage.)*

MR GARDINER. And here we are. What do you make of the county, Lizzy?

ELIZABETH. Very fine – what a mixture of wild and tamed scenery – the rugged peaks, and the tailored gardens of Chatsworth.

MR GARDINER. Now, what do you say to our visiting Pemberley? It is not directly in our way, but only a mile or two out of it.

ELIZABETH. Do *you* particularly want to see it, aunt?

MRS GARDINER. I should have thought that *you* might – having heard so much about it. Mr Wickham spent his childhood there, you know!

(A pause. **ELIZABETH** *is thinking of* **MR DARCY**, *not* **MR WICKHAM**.*)*

ELIZABETH. I should feel awkward, having no business there, and no invitation.

MRS GARDINER. We visited Blenheim and Chatsworth – there was no awkwardness there.

*(***SERVANT*** *enters right carrying some boxes/ sheets.)*

Let's ask the servant. Hannah – do they welcome visitors at Pemberley?

HANNAH. Yes, ma'am, the Housekeeper will show you inside the house, and the gardens are very fine – my brother is an under-gardener there.

ELIZABETH. Are the family at home at present?

HANNAH. No, Miss, the master's in London.

ELIZABETH. Then I think we may visit Pemberley.

MR GARDINER. Excellent!

> (*Lights down and link music.* **ELIZABETH,** **MR GARDINER** *and* **MRS GARDINER** *turn and walk upstage.*)

Scene Five – Pemberley – Exterior and Interior

> (*Lights up and birdsong as* **ELIZABETH**, **MR GARDINER** *and* **MRS GARDINER** *turn to walk downstage.* **ELIZABETH** *as we know is a great walker, but* **MR GARDINER** *is a bit out of condition and he's mopping his brow.* **MRS GARDINER** *is younger than her husband and loves a walk.*)

MR GARDINER. Well – I confess I had – no idea – Pemberley had such extensive grounds!

MRS GARDINER. Courage, my dear – just round the next bend and we will see it.

> (**ELIZABETH**, **MR GARDINER** *and* **MRS GARDINER** *all pause, looking offstage at Pemberley.*)

ELIZABETH. Oh!

MRS GARDINER. What do you think, Lizzy? Is it superior to Rosings?

ELIZABETH. Oh, far superior. Rosings is a stark modern building. This house nestles into the landscape as if it had always belonged here! I like it very much.

MRS GARDINER. I think one would put up with a great deal, in order to be mistress of Pemberley.

MR GARDINER. And from what I hear, the mistress of Pemberley *will* have to put up with a great deal.

MRS GARDINER. Well she's not likely to be anyone *we* know. Shall we apply to the housekeeper to show us around?

Inside Pemberley

(**MRS REYNOLDS** *enters right and* **ELIZABETH,
MR GARDINER** *and* **MRS GARDINER** *cross to*
MRS REYNOLDS.)

MRS REYNOLDS. This way, please.

MRS GARDINER. This is very kind of you.

MRS REYNOLDS. Not at all, ma'am, it's a pleasure to show
the house off to visitors.

(*They all stroll across stage and* **MRS
REYNOLDS** *indicates offstage to the various
rooms/areas of Pemberley.*)

This is where Mrs Darcy used to write her letters in the
morning; it was her favourite room. And here we have
the music room...

ELIZABETH. What a beautiful room.

MRS REYNOLDS. The pianoforte arrived only yesterday,
sent on from London, for Miss Georgiana. If you look
through this window, there's a fine prospect of the park,
down to the lake.

(**MR GARDINER** *and* **MRS GARDINER,**
ELIZABETH *all take a look offstage to where*
MRS REYNOLDS *is indicating.*)

MR GARDINER. Magnificent.

(**ELIZABETH** *turns away towards the
audience.*)

ELIZABETH. Of all this I might have been mistress.

MR GARDINER. Your master is from home, I understand?

MRS REYNOLDS. Yes, sir, but we expect him here
tomorrow, with a party of friends and Miss Georgiana.

(**ELIZABETH** *starts.*)

If you'd walk this way into the gallery...this is Miss Georgiana, painted a year ago.

> (**MRS REYNOLDS** *indicates portraits offstage. There are three portraits, first is* **GEORGIANA**, *next is* **MR WICKHAM** *and then* **MR DARCY**. *All look up at the portraits.*)

ELIZABETH. She's beautiful.

MRS REYNOLDS. Yes, and sweet-natured too, like her brother.

> (**MR GARDINER** *raises his eyebrow at* **MRS GARDINER**. **MRS REYNOLDS** *walks on past Wickham's portrait.*)

MR GARDINER. Is that so?

MRS GARDINER. Look at this one, Lizzy! This reminds me very much of someone we know!

> (**ELIZABETH** *and* **MR GARDINER** *go and look up at the portrait of* **MR WICKHAM**. **MRS REYNOLDS** *joins them.*)

MRS REYNOLDS. That one, madam? He was the son of old Mr Darcy's steward, Mr Wickham. He has gone into the army now and turned out very wild, they say. *(She walks on.)* And here is my master.

> *(They all look at the imaginary portrait of* **MR DARCY**.*)

MRS GARDINER. What do you think, Lizzy? Is it like him?

ELIZABETH. Yes – very like.

MRS REYNOLDS. Does the young lady know my master?

ELIZABETH. Yes; a little.

MRS REYNOLDS. He is a handsome gentleman, is he not, Miss?

ELIZABETH. Very handsome.

MRS REYNOLDS. I'm sure I know none so handsome. Or so kind.

MR GARDINER. Indeed.

MRS REYNOLDS. I've never heard a cross word from him, and I've known him since he was four-years-old. He's the best master and the best landlord – ask any of his servants or his tenants. Some call him proud, but that's only because he don't rattle on like other young men. You should see him with Miss Georgiana, so affectionate and tenderhearted!

MR GARDINER. A paragon of men, then.

MRS REYNOLDS Indeed he is, sir.

(They've reached the end of their tour.)

MRS GARDINER. Thank you, Mrs Reynolds.

MRS REYNOLDS. A pleasure, ma'am. Goodbye.

*(**MRS REYNOLDS** exits right.)*

MRS GARDINER. What now?

ELIZABETH. I'd like to walk a little in the park.

MR GARDINER. We'll see you by the carriage, then.

*(**MR GARDINER** and **MRS GARDINER** exit right. Sound of a peacock as **ELIZABETH** strolls upstage.)*

Exterior Pemberley

(**ELIZABETH** *takes a deep breath, then turns... and comes face-to-face with* **MR DARCY** *who has entered right.* **MR DARCY** *is dripping wet, especially his shirt and hair, he is carrying his jacket. They face each other centre.*)

ELIZABETH. Mr Darcy.

MR DARCY. Miss Bennet! (*They stare at each other in total bewilderment and panic.*) I ...

ELIZABETH. I did not expect to see you, sir. We understood you were in London.

MR DARCY. I returned a day early. Excuse me. – Your parents are in good health?

ELIZABETH. Yes, they are very well, I thank you sir.

MR DARCY. I am glad to hear it. How long have you been in this part of the country?

ELIZABETH. But two days, sir.

MR DARCY. And where are you staying?

ELIZABETH. The inn at Lambton. (*Pause.*) You're all wet.

MR DARCY. I – went for a swim. In the lake.

ELIZABETH. Of course.

MR DARCY. And your family are well?

ELIZABETH. Very well, thank you.

MR DARCY. Excuse me. (*And he strides away quickly exiting right.*)

ELIZABETH. Oh, how I wish we had never come! What must he think of me now?

(*Lights down and link music.*)

Scene Six – The Inn At Lambton

(**MR GARDINER** *and* **MRS GARDINER** *enter and sit right.* **ELIZABETH** *crosses to join them, taking off her cape, and* **HANNAH** *takes off with her.* **HANNAH** *enters with three glasses containing wine. They all take a drink.*)

MRS GARDINER. Thank you, Hannah.

MR GARDINER. So, you encountered the great man himself! We saw you talking to someone and wondered who it was.

(**HANNAH**, *collects the empty glasses. Curtsies and exits right.* **MRS GARDINER** *indicates her thanks to* **HANNAH**.)

ELIZABETH. It was mortifying! I felt like a trespasser.

MRS GARDINER. Was he displeased to see you?

ELIZABETH. I don't know – he seemed as shocked as I was. Oh, can we not leave this place as soon as possible?

MR GARDINER. Of course, if that's what you wish. Where next? Matlock Bath?

(**HANNAH** *enters right.*)

HANNAH. If you please, Miss Bennet, there's a lady and two gentlemen to see you.

(**HANNAH** *stands back.* **MR DARCY, MR BINGLEY** *and* **GEORGIANA** *enter right.* **GEORGIANA** *wearing a cape/coat.*)

MR DARCY. Miss Bennet, will you allow me to introduce my sister Georgiana?

(**ELIZABETH** *and* **GEORGIANA** *curtsy to one another.*)

ELIZABETH. It's a pleasure to meet you, Miss, Mr Darcy – my aunt and uncle Mr and Mrs Gardiner – Mr Darcy and Mr Bingley.

> *(General bowing and curtsies and how d'you doing.)*

MR BINGLEY. Miss Bennet, I can't tell you how delighted I am to see you again! How are you? But I can see, you're very well. Pray tell me – are *all* your sisters still at Longbourn?

ELIZABETH. All except my youngest – she is at Brighton.

MR BINGLEY. It seems too long – it *is* too long – since we were all together.

ELIZABETH. It must be several months.

> *(***GEORGIANA*** whispers in ***MR DARCY****'s ear.)*

MR BINGLEY. It is more than eight months. We have not met since the 26th November, when we were all dancing together at Netherfield.

MR DARCY. Miss Bennet, my sister has a request she would make of you.

GEORGIANA. *(She's shy.)* Miss Bennet, my brother and I would be honoured if you – and your aunt and uncle – would be our guests for dinner at Pemberley. Would tomorrow evening be convenient?

ELIZABETH. Thank you – you are very kind.

MR DARCY. Till tomorrow, then.

> *(***MR DARCY***, **MR BINGLEY** and **GEORGIANA** exit left. ***GEORGIANA*** takes her cape off.)*

MR GARDINER. Well. What about *that*?

> *(Lights down, link music. Set chairs left, piano and stool for Pemberley.*

MRS GARDINER *and* **ELIZABETH** *exit right and take off capes.* **MR GARDINER** *follows.)*

Scene Seven – Pemberley – Interior

(**ELIZABETH, MR GARDINER** *and* **MRS GARDINER** *re-enter right with* **ELIZABETH** *going to the piano**. **MRS GARDINER** *sits,* **MR GARDINER** *stands beside her.* **GEORGIANA** *enters left and stands next to* **ELIZABETH** *at the piano as she turns the pages of music.* **MR DARCY, MR BINGLEY** *enter left and stand.* **MISS BINGLEY** *enters left and sits. If no doubling,* **MRS HURST** *enters left and sits. Lights up full stage.* **ELIZABETH** *comes to the end of her piano piece. Applause, enthusiastic from* **MR BINGLEY,** *sincere from* **MR DARCY,** *limp from* **MISS BINGLEY** *and* **MRS HURST.**)

MR BINGLEY. Beautifully played, Miss Bennet!

ELIZABETH. It is a beautiful instrument.

GEORGIANA. It was a birthday gift from my brother. He is so good to me, and really I don't deserve it.

ELIZABETH. *He* thinks you do, and you know he is never wrong! Now it is your turn to play. Come, I insist.

GEORGIANA. In front of all these people? Very well, I will play, but please don't make me sing.

ELIZABETH. If you wish.

(**GEORGIANA** *sits at the piano, and as she starts to play*,* **ELIZABETH** *moves slightly away but nearer to the waspish* **MISS BINGLEY.**)

---

* A licence to produce *Pride and Prejudice* does not include a performance licence for any third-party or copyrighted music. Licensees should create an original composition or use music in the public domain. For further information, please see the Music and Third-Party Materials Use Note on page iii.

MISS BINGLEY. Pray, Miss Elizabeth, are the militia still quartered at Meryton?

ELIZABETH. No, they are encamped at Brighton for the summer.

MISS BINGLEY. That must be a great loss for your family!

ELIZABETH. We are enduring it as best we can, Miss Bingley.

MISS BINGLEY. I should have thought *one* gentleman's absence might have caused particular pangs.

ELIZABETH. I can't think what you mean.

MISS BINGLEY. Mr *Wickham* was a particular favourite of yours, I think?

> (**GEORGIANA** *plays a bum note,* **MR DARCY** *notices and starts towards* **GEORGIANA** *in concern.* **ELIZABETH** *darts to* **GEORGIANA***'s side.* **MR DARCY** *stops.*)

ELIZABETH. I am so sorry, I've been neglecting you – how can you play with no one to turn the pages?

> (**ELIZABETH** *turns a page and* **GEORGIANA** *recovers her composure and plays on.*)

MR DARCY. *(Mouths it.)* Thank you.

> (**GEORGIANA** *plays on, while* **MR DARCY** *and* **ELIZABETH** *gaze at each other across the room, till the end of the scene. Lights fade down slowly while music continues into scene change.* **MR DARCY, MR BINGLEY, MISS BINGLEY, MRS HURST** *and* **GEORGIANA** *exit left.*)

Scene Eight – The Inn at Lambton

> (**ELIZABETH**, **MR GARDINER** *and* **MRS GARDINER** *cross to right. Lights up right.*)

MR GARDINER. Mr Darcy was all politeness – showed me all the best fishing spots – and Mr Bingley, too, such an amiable gentleman – we are invited to join them again today, but perhaps it wouldn't be wise to take them at their word – what do you think?

ELIZABETH. I don't know what to advise.

MRS GARDINER. Suppose we confine ourselves to Lambton for the morning at least – I have a fancy to walk to the church.

ELIZABETH. I shall be happy to walk with you.

> (**HANNAH** *enters right with a letter.*)

HANNAH. A letter for you, Miss Bennet.

ELIZABETH. Thank you. It's from Jane! Will you excuse me from our walk – I must read Jane's letter.

MRS GARDINER. We'll see you later, then.

> (**MR GARDINER** *and* **MRS GARDINER** *exit right.* **ELIZABETH** *opens letter and starts to read – the contents are very shocking!*)

ELIZABETH. Oh no!

> (**ELIZABETH** *reads on, feverishly, stands, clutching her chest. And* **HANNAH** *shows in* **MR DARCY**.)

HANNAH. Mr Darcy, Miss. (*She exits right.*)

MR DARCY. Forgive me – I couldn't wait to –

ELIZABETH. I beg your pardon – I must find Mr and Mrs Gardiner, on business that must not be delayed!

MR DARCY. Good God! What is the matter? I won't detain you for a moment, but let me, or the servant, go after Mr and Mrs Gardiner, you are not well enough – hallo there!

(**HANNAH** *reappears.*)

Go and fetch Mr and Mrs Gardiner immediately – they are walking towards –

ELIZABETH. The church.

MR DARCY. The church.

HANNAH. Yes, sir, at once. (*She exits right.*)

MR DARCY. You are ill. What can I do? A glass of wine? Can I get you one?

ELIZABETH. No – I am quite well. It is – I have just had the most dreadful news!

MR DARCY. What is it? Your parents?

ELIZABETH. No. (*She's in an agony of doubt about whether to tell him, then decides.*)

ELIZABETH. The world will know soon enough. My youngest sister, who was at Brighton, has left her friends – has eloped – *with Mr Wickham*!

MR DARCY. But is it certain? Absolutely certain?

ELIZABETH. Yes! They left Brighton together on Sunday night. They were traced as far as London, but no further. My father has gone to London, and Jane writes to beg Mr Gardiner's assistance in finding her. But what can be done? How is such a man to be worked upon? And to think that I had the means to warn her against him! I have not the smallest hope. And our whole family is disgraced.

MR DARCY. I can see you have long been desiring my absence. I wish I could comfort you – but I won't torment you with vain wishes.

ELIZABETH. Please – would you conceal the unhappy truth as long as possible?

MR DARCY. Of course. But I have stayed too long. I shall leave you now. Goodbye.

ELIZABETH. Goodbye.

> (**MR DARCY** *exits right.*)

I shall never see him again.

> (*Lights fade, link music. Scene change, move chairs, take off the piano.* **ELIZABETH** *exits right.*)

Scene Nine – Longbourn

(**MRS BENNET** *sits on a chair. Lights up stage.*
ELIZABETH *enters right followed closely by*
MR GARDINER. *They hurry across to meet*
JANE *as she enters left.* **ELIZABETH** *and* **JANE**
embrace.)

JANE. Oh, Lizzy, I am very glad to see you!

ELIZABETH. Is there any news?

JANE. No – Papa is still in London. Mama has been asking
for you every five minutes.

ELIZABETH. And how is she?

JANE. She has not left her room.

ELIZABETH. And you look pale. Oh, Jane, what you must
have gone through!

JANE. I feel much better for seeing you.

ELIZABETH. We had better go to Mamma.

(**MRS BENNET** *is half collapsed in a chair,*
in a state of nerves. **ELIZABETH** *crosses to*
MRS BENNET *and kisses her and sits.* **JANE**
and **MR GARDINER** *follow and stand.*)

MRS BENNET. Oh, Lizzy, oh brother, we are ruined forever!
If only your father had taken us all to Brighton, this
would never have happened! I blame those Forsters for
not looking after our girl!

ELIZABETH. Mamma –

MRS BENNET. And now Mr Bennet's gone in search of
Wickham, and I'm sure he'll fight him, and be killed,
and then where will we all be? Those Collinses will
turn us out of the house before he is cold in his grave!

MR GARDINER. Sister, calm yourself. I will see Mr Bennet tomorrow in Gracechurch Street, and then we can discuss what's to be done.

MRS BENNET. Yes, yes – you must find them out, and make them marry! But above all, don't let Mr Bennet fight!

JANE. Mama, I'm sure Papa does not intend to fight.

MRS BENNET. Yes, he does, and get himself killed! You must make them marry, brother! But tell Lydia she is not to give any directions about wedding clothes till she has consulted me, for she does *not know the best warehouses*!! Oh, my nerves have been in such a flutter, I have had such trembling's and spasms and pains, I can get no rest, night or day!

> (**MARY** *and* **KITTY** *enter and cross to centre. They are joined by* **ELIZABETH** *and* **JANE**. **MRS BENNET** *stays seated and freezes.*)

MARY. This is indeed a most unfortunate affair. And will probably be much talked of.

ELIZABETH. Yes, thank you, Mary, I think we've all grasped that.

MARY. But we must stem the tide of malice, and pour into each other's wounded bosoms the balm of sisterly consolation.

> (*"Eh?" Thinks* **KITTY**, *"what's all that about?"*)

JANE. Thank you, Mary.

MARY. Unhappy as this event is for Lydia, we must draw this useful lesson from it: loss of virtue in a female is irretrievable.

KITTY. I don't see that Lydia has done anything so very dreadful!

ELIZABETH. Kitty! She has ruined us all!

(**ELIZABETH** *crosses downstage furious.* **JANE** *follows her.* **MARY** *and* **KITTY** *cross to* **MRS BENNET** *upstage.* **ELIZABETH** *and* **JANE** *are alone.*)

JANE. Lizzy. Did you really mean what you said to Kitty?

ELIZABETH. I shouldn't have said it. I was angry and upset. It does no good to dwell on it. And it's not poor Kitty's fault.

JANE. But it is true, isn't it? You, and I, and Mary and Kitty, have been affected by this – escapade of Lydia's. Our chances of making a good marriage have been damaged.

ELIZABETH. Our chances of making a good marriage were never great. Now they are nonexistent. Mr Darcy made that very clear to me.

JANE. Mr *Darcy*? Does *he* know of our troubles?

ELIZABETH. He happened upon me as I was reading your letter. He made it very clear that he wanted nothing more to do with me. He will not be renewing his addresses to me, and he will make sure that Mr Bingley will keep clear of you.

JANE. I never expected any more of Mr Bingley, Lizzy. I am reconciled to that. But – did you hope that Mr Darcy would renew his addresses to you?

ELIZABETH. No – I never sought them.

JANE. But – you think he is still in love with you?

ELIZABETH. I don't know that, he was two days ago. I do know that now he doesn't want anything to do with me, or any of us.

(*Pause. Then* **KITTY** *runs across to point offstage.*)

KITTY. Oh, Lord, look who's coming!

JANE. Who, Kitty?

KITTY. Mr Collins! I'm going to hide in the garden!

> *(**KITTY** exits. **ELIZABETH**, **JANE** and **MARY** assemble themselves to receive **MR COLLINS**. He is carrying a bible.)*

JANE. Mr Collins.

MR COLLINS. Cousin Jane, Cousin Elizabeth, Cousin Mary. I had hoped to condole with your poor father and mother.

JANE. Our father is in London, sir, and our mother is too unwell to leave her room.

MR COLLINS. Ah. Ah. Then I must condole with you. This is a grievous situation indeed, and I am very sorry for you.

JANE. Thank you, sir.

MARY. It has often been said: a friend in need is a friend indeed.

MR COLLINS. Very true. Your situation could hardly be worse. The *death* of your sister would be a blessing compared to this.

ELIZABETH. Really, sir –

MR COLLINS. I am inclined to think that her disposition must be naturally bad, though her upbringing has been deplorably lax. Be that as it may – this false step by one sister must sadly damage the prospects of the others. For who, as Lady Catherine says, who will connect themselves to such a family?

ELIZABETH. *(Getting closer to **MR COLLINS**.)* Who indeed? And perhaps you might think it unwise to stay here any longer yourself.

MR COLLINS. Well, well – perhaps you are right, cousin Elizabeth.

ELIZABETH. A clergyman cannot be too careful, you know.

MR COLLINS. Your thoughtfulness does you credit, cousin Elizabeth. I am truly very, very sorry for you all! Well, ah...yes.

(**MR COLLINS** *backs out right.*)

ELIZABETH. Insufferable man!

JANE. I suppose he means well.

ELIZABETH. You suppose wrong. He came to enjoy our misfortunes and rejoice at his own happy lot.

MARY. *I* think it was very kind of him to come and console us.

(**KITTY** *enters slowly to check if Mr Collins has gone.*)

KITTY. Has he gone?

ELIZABETH. Yes.

KITTY. Good.

ELIZABETH. And forever, with any luck.

(**MRS BENNET** *calls from offstage.*)

MRS BENNET. Girls! Girls! Was that not Mr Collins?

JANE. I'll go to her.

(**MRS BENNET** *is still in her chair.*)

MRS BENNET. Come to lord it over us all, no doubt, and to inspect our house, which *he* will have as soon as Mr Wickham kills your father!

JANE. Mamma, Mr Wickham isn't going to –

MRS BENNET. Mrs Phillips has been here, and Meryton is nothing but talk of Mr Wickham, of bills unpaid, and gaming debts, and drunken routs – she said there was scarce one tradesman in the town whose daughter hadn't been meddled with! And now he's meddling with our dearest girl! The foul fiend! Well, he shall be discovered and made to marry her!

JANE. Mamma, calm yourself!

MRS BENNET. How can I calm myself when my dear girl is in the arms of a foul fiend? I always suspected him! Too smooth and plausible by half! But would anybody listen to me? And now we are all ruined! Oh, my poor, poor Lydia!

> *(Lights down, link music.* **JANE**, **ELIZABETH**, **KITTY** *and* **MARY** *stay with* **MRS BENNET** *and freeze.)*

Scene Ten – A Room in London

(**LYDIA** *enters right and stands/sits by the window and is looking out and humming a song.* **MR WICKHAM** *enters and sits and he is looking a bit the worse for wear, totting up figures in a notebook on the desk/writing slope.* **MR WICKHAM** *jacket is undone. Lights up.*)

LYDIA. When shall we travel to Hertfordshire, my love?

MR WICKHAM. Come away from the window, dear. We'll go as soon as I've settled my affairs. These things take time. You're not unhappy?

LYDIA. Me? Lord, no! It's just I can't wait to see my mother's face! And my sisters! How we'll laugh! Oh, I wish we could go out into town, and be seen at plays and assemblies. Can we go to a play? Dear Wickham?

MR WICKHAM. Ah, no, dear – too risky.

LYDIA. Shall we to bed again then?

MR WICKHAM. I am a little tired, my dear.

LYDIA. Lord! It makes me laugh to think that I have done what none of my sisters have! Seventeen times!

MR WICKHAM. Do come away from the window, dear.

LYDIA. Oh, I want to hug you as tight as tight!

(**LYDIA** *goes to* **MR WICKHAM** *and hugs him from behind.*)

MR WICKHAM. Please don't, dear.

(*It's clear* **LYDIA** *is a bit much for* **MR WICKHAM.** **LYDIA** *and* **MR WICKHAM** *stay and freeze. Lights down right, link music.*)

Scene Eleven – Longbourn

(*Lights up left.* **MRS BENNET**, **ELIZABETH**, **JANE**, **KITTY** *and* **MARY** *are still left.* **MAID** *enters and gives a letter to* **JANE**.)

JANE. Mamma! Father is coming home!

MRS BENNET. Does he bring Lydia?

JANE. No –

(**MRS BENNET** *lets out a wail.*)

They have not yet found out where she is – my uncle Mr Gardiner will continue the search.

MRS BENNET. But who will fight Mr Wickham, and bring Lydia home? Oh, Jane, Jane, fetch my smelling salts! I feel my faintness coming upon me!

(**MAID** *comes on left with smelling salts and gives them to* **MRS BENNET**. *Lights down.* **BUTLER** *brings on a chair and sets downstage for* **MR BENNET**. **MRS BENNET** *exits left.* **JANE**, **KITTY** *and* **MARY** *stay. Lights up downstage as* **MR BENNET** *enters right looking tired.* **ELIZABETH** *goes across to greet him.*)

MR BENNET. Not now, Lizzy.

ELIZABETH. Come. Sit down. You must be exhausted.

(**MR BENNET** *lets her lead him to a chair.* **MAID** *enters left to attend to* **MR BENNET**.)

Shall I bring you some tea?

(**JANE**, **KITTY** *and* **MARY** *cross to join and stand by* **MR BENNET**.)

MR BENNET. If you would – but I don't deserve this solicitude. If I am suffering, who should suffer but myself? It has been my own doing, and I ought to feel it.

> (**ELIZABETH** *indicates to* **MAID** *for tea.* **MAID** *exits.*)

JANE. You mustn't be so severe upon yourself, Papa.

MR BENNET. No, Jane, let me once in my life feel how much I have been to blame. I am not afraid of being overpowered by the impression. It will pass soon enough.

ELIZABETH. Do you suppose them to be still in London?

> (**MAID** *enters left with tray, cup and saucer. Offers it to* **ELIZABETH** *who takes the cup and gives it to* **MR BENNET**.)

MR BENNET. Yes; where else can they be so well concealed?

KITTY. And Lydia always wanted to go to London!

MR BENNET. She is happy, then. Let us count our blessings. Lizzy, I bear you no ill will for being justified in your advice. *(He sighs.)* Where is your mother?

ELIZABETH. She has not left her room.

MR BENNET. Perhaps I should do the same. I'll sit in my library in a nightgown and powdered cap, and give as much trouble as I can, till it's Kitty's turn to run away!

KITTY. I'm not going to run away, Papa, and if you let me go to Brighton, I'd behave better than Lydia did.

MR BENNET. What? *You* go to Brighton? I wouldn't trust you within ten miles of it! No, Kitty, I have learnt my lesson. No officer is ever to enter my house again, there will be no dancing, and you are not permitted to stir out of doors till you can prove you have spent ten minutes of every day in a rational manner!

(**KITTY** *bursts into tears.* **JANE** *comforts her.*)

Well, well, don't upset yourself. If you're a good girl for the next ten years, I'll take you to a review. How's that?

(**KITTY** *runs off sobbing.*)

She'll get over it. *(He gets up.)* If anyone wants me, I shall be in my library. But I don't wish to be disturbed.

(*Lights down, link music as* **MR BENNET** *exits upstage with his cup.* **BUTLER/MAID** *enters and takes chairs off.* **JANE**, **ELIZABETH** *and* **MARY** *exit left.*)

Scene Twelve – A Room in London

(Lights up right. **MR WICKHAM** *morose, with a beer bottle. Mr Wickham's jacket is now off and on back of chair.* **LYDIA** *is restless, pacing up and down.)*

LYDIA. You're very dull this evening, dearest! I hope you're not getting tired of me!

MR WICKHAM. Of course not, dearest girl.

LYDIA. I could have had my pick of all the young officers, you know! And I chose you! Aren't you flattered?

MR WICKHAM. I am thrilled to the core.

*(***MR WICKHAM** *actually sounds a bit fed up.* **LYDIA** *goes over to the window.)*

Don't show yourself at the window, dear.

LYDIA. Oh, piffle! No one knows us here. What a funny mixture of people one sees in London! Lord! I wouldn't wear a bonnet like that for fifty pounds! Oh, there's a dog with a big piece of meat, and a man chasing him!

MR WICKHAM. How many more times – come *away*!

LYDIA. Lord! What's *he* doing here?

MR WICKHAM. What?

LYDIA. What a joke!

MR WICKHAM. What? Who is it?

LYDIA. You'll never guess!

MR WICKHAM. Then tell me, damn it!

LYDIA. Mr Darcy!

(Lights fade as dramatic music plays.* **WICKHAM** *and* **LYDIA** *exit right.)*

---

* A licence to produce *Pride and Prejudice* does not include a performance licence for any third-party or copyrighted recordings. Licensees should create their own

Scene Thirteen – Longbourn

(MR BENNET enters left. KITTY runs on with a letter from MR GARDINER.)

KITTY. Papa! Papa! An express letter from Uncle Gardiner!

MR BENNET. Give it here. Thank you. That's all. Off with you!

(KITTY exits left. MR BENNET sits down to read it. While he's doing that, ELIZABETH and JANE enter, one from each side. They don't want to interrupt him, so pace about, but they are dying to know what's in the letter. Finally, MR BENNET folds up the letter. ELIZABETH and JANE move closer to MR BENNET.)

Well, Jane. Well, Lizzy.

JANE. Is it good news?

ELIZABETH. Have they been found?

JANE. Are they married?

MR BENNET. They have been found, and they are not married. But they will be, if I make certain promises.

ELIZABETH. What promises?

MR BENNET. If I guarantee Lydia will have her share of the five thousand due to her when we are gone, plus one hundred pounds a year...

ELIZABETH. And that is all? No more than that?

MR BENNET. It seems that Mr Wickham's circumstances are not as desperate as we thought. Mr Gardiner suggests they be married from Gracechurch Street. He will take care of all the arrangements.

ELIZABETH. Is it possible that Mr Wickham will take her for so little?

JANE. He is not so undeserving after all, then.

MR BENNET. I doubt that. But there are two things I would like to know: one is, how much money your uncle has laid down, and the other, how I am ever to pay him.

JANE. Money? My uncle? What do you mean?

MR BENNET. I mean that no one in his right mind would marry Lydia on so slight a temptation as a hundred a year.

ELIZABETH. Oh! It must be my uncle's doing! He must have paid Mr Wickham's debts, and more! What a generous man he is! But has he put himself in difficulties? A small sum would not be enough.

MR BENNET. No. Mr Wickham's a fool, if he takes her with any less than ten thousand pounds.

ELIZABETH. Ten thousand? How is half such a sum to be repaid?

MR BENNET. How indeed? Leave me now, girls, for I must write my reply.

> (**MR BENNET** *exits upstage*. **MRS BENNET** *explodes onto the stage, fully recovered to robust good health*. **KITTY** *and* **MARY** *follow and enter left*.)

MRS BENNET. Girls! Girls! What wonderful news! Dear Lydia! Dear Wickham! I always knew it would be so! People were saying all sorts of things about him, but I would have none of it, and I was right all the time! My dearest Lydia! Married at sixteen! But the wedding clothes! I must write to my sister Mrs Gardiner about them directly! No expense should be spared! Mrs Wickham! How well that sounds! Kitty, order the carriage, I'll go to Meryton as soon as I am dressed, to tell Mrs Phillips and Mrs Long and Sir William Lucas the happy news!

> (**MRS BENNET** *exits left.* **KITTY** *and* **MARY** *stay upstage and freeze.* **JANE** *and* **ELIZABETH** *cross downstage to be together alone.*)

JANE. So, a happy outcome after all!

ELIZABETH. You call it a happy outcome? It is not as bad as the one we feared – but could Lydia be happy with such a man?

JANE. We must hope that marriage will reform him. I believe it will.

ELIZABETH. I wish I could share your belief. *(After a pause.)* I wish I had never spoken a word of Lydia's affairs to Mr Darcy!

JANE. Don't distress yourself – I'm sure he will respect your confidence.

ELIZABETH. I'm sure he will. That is not what distresses me.

JANE. What then?

ELIZABETH. I don't know! How he must be congratulating himself on his lucky escape! And how he must despise me now!

JANE. But Lizzy, you never sought his love. Why should you care now?

ELIZABETH. I don't know! I can't explain it! But I cannot bear the thought that he is alive in the world, and thinking ill of me.

> (**KITTY** *rushes across to point offstage.* **MR** *and* **MRS BENNET** *enter left to welcome* **LYDIA** *and* **MR WICKHAM.** **MARY** *crosses into the scene.* **ELIZABETH** *and* **JANE** *join* **MARY** *left.*)

KITTY. Mamma! Lizzy! Jane! They're here!

> (**LYDIA** *and* **MR WICKHAM** *come onstage, arm in arm.* **MR BENNET** *holds back: he's not in a mood to be welcoming.* **MRS BENNET** *rushes at* **LYDIA** *and embraces her.* **KITTY** *and* **MARY ELIZABETH** *left.*)

MRS BENNET. Oh, my dear, dear girl!

LYDIA. Lord! It seems an age since I was last at Longbourn! And here you all are, just the same! Haven't I caught a handsome husband!

MRS BENNET. Indeed you have! You're very welcome, Mr Wickham!

> (**MRS BENNET** *gives him a big kiss too, and he smirks, not in the least embarrassed.*)

LYDIA. I'm sure you must all envy me!

MARY. I do not.

LYDIA. You must all go to Brighton, that's the place to get husbands!

KITTY. Who was at your wedding, Lydia? Did all the officers come?

LYDIA. No, I was cross about that, but they said there wasn't time for a big wedding, *(To* **ELIZABETH** *only.)* there was only my aunt and uncle and Mr Darcy.

> (**MR BENNET** *and* **MRS BENNET**, **MARY**, **KITTY** *and* **JANE** *all turn away from* **LYDIA** *and* **ELIZABETH**.)

ELIZABETH. Mr Darcy??

LYDIA. Yes! Oh, Lord! *(She puts her hand to her mouth and giggles.)* I wasn't supposed to say anything – well, it's out now! Yes, he arranged everything and paid off dear Mr Wickham's debts – I expect he was sorry for the way he treated my poor Wickham in the past! Well, shall we go in? I'm starving!

> (**LYDIA** *crosses to the rest of the* **BENNETS** *leaving* **ELIZABETH** *and* **MR WICKHAM** *alone.*)

ELIZABETH. I hear you are leaving the militia, and joining a regiment in the North.

MR WICKHAM. Yes; I am sorry we shall be so far from Longbourn. I so enjoyed our conversations. I sometimes think – if things had turned out differently...

ELIZABETH. I am very glad they didn't.

MR WICKHAM. Well, perhaps you are right.

> (*Time passing, lights down and link music as everyone walks upstage. Lights up as* **LYDIA** *and* **MR WICKHAM** *walk forward arm in arm.* **MR BENNET** *and* **MRS BENNET,** **ELIZABETH, JANE, KITTY** *and* **MARY** *all follow downstage.*)

MRS BENNET. Oh, must you go again so soon?

MR WICKHAM. The regiment awaits, Ma'am. If I had my way, I'd never leave Longbourn.

MRS BENNET. Dear Wickham! You will write won't you, Lydia?

LYDIA. Well, I don't know – we married women don't have much time for writing! My sisters can write to me – it's not as if they have anything to do!

MRS BENNET. (*To* **MR WICKHAM.**) Take care of my dear girl!

MR WICKHAM. I shall. And now, duty calls me away – farewell, let us not say adieu, but as the French say, au revoir!

(**LYDIA** *and* **MR WICKHAM** *exit right.*)

MR BENNET. Well, there they go. And I, for one, cannot say I'm sorry to see the back of them.

MRS BENNET. Oh, Mr Bennet! How can you say such a thing, when you know you don't mean it!

(**MR BENNET** *and* **MRS BENNET** *go to sit,* **ELIZABETH**, **JANE**, **KITTY** *and* **MARY** *stand around them left.* **MAID** *enters with a note/ letter.* **KITTY** *open the letter and announces –)*

KITTY. Mamma! You'll never guess what! Mr Bingley is returned to Netherfield!

(**KITTY** *and* **MARY** *exit left.* **ELIZABETH** *and* **JANE** *cross downstage to be alone.* **MR BENNET** *and* **MRS BENNET** *stay seated and freeze.)*

(**JANE** *walks downstage with* **ELIZABETH**.*)*

JANE. I assure you, Lizzy, this news does not affect me.

ELIZABETH. *(Smiling.)* I'm not contradicting you.

JANE. I feel it in your gaze. But I am perfectly calm. One thing I am glad of – it seems to be only a shooting party, he has brought no ladies with him. We shall not see him often. Not that I'm afraid for myself – but I dread other people's remarks.

ELIZABETH. Then I shall make none. And after all, it's a shame if a man can't come to his own house to shoot his own birds without creating a commotion.

JANE. That's what I think, Lizzy.

(**ELIZABETH** *smiles.)*

Stop it, Lizzy.

*(**JANE** and **ELIZABETH** cross upstage and mime chatting/freeze during next exchange. **MR BENNET** and **MRS BENNET** are seated left.)*

MRS BENNET. As soon as Bingley comes, you must wait upon him, my dear.

MR BENNET. I shall do no such thing. If he wants to see us, he knows where we live.

MRS BENNET. Well, I am determined he shall dine here. Even if he has behaved so ill to our Jane.

MR BENNET. Then anything I say or do is beside the point.

MRS BENNET. Oh, Mr Bennet! I wish you would not be so tiresome!

*(**MR BENNET** smiles and exits left. **KITTY** enters left and looks offstage as if looking out of a window.)*

KITTY. Mamma! He's coming! *(She peers out.)* Well, somebody's coming. *(**MRS BENNET** joins **KITTY** as they both peer out.)* It is him! And someone else!

MRS BENNET. Who else?

KITTY. I think it's that man who came before. That tall grumpy one.

MRS BENNET. Yes, it is! – Mr Darcy, horrid creature! Well, I'll be civil for Bingley's sake. Jane! Jane!

*(**JANE** and **ELIZABETH** cross to **MRS BENNET** and **KITTY**.)*

There you are! Stand up straight, Jane. Pull your shoulders back – you have a fine figure if only you'd make the most of it –

*(**MAID** enters right.)*

MAID. Mr Bingley and Mr Darcy Ma'am. *(Steps back, curtsies and exits right.)*

> *(**MR BINGLEY** and **MR DARCY** enter right, **MR BINGLEY** all smiles, **MR DARCY** very serious. All curtsy and bow. **MRS BENNET** starts talking and continues almost without a breath.)*

MRS BENNET. Mr Bingley, you are very welcome! We were afraid we'd lost you for ever! And Mr Darcy you are welcome too.

> *(**MRS BENNET**'s has a definite change of tone for the last sentence. **MRS BENNET** rambles on, **MR BINGLEY** is smiling at **JANE** and she is reciprocating – **MR DARCY** and **ELIZABETH** are not so comfortable, but very conscious of each other.)*

Ring the bell for tea, Kitty!

> *(**KITTY** nods and exits left.)*

Well, there have been many changes since you were last here – my youngest daughter Lydia is married! Perhaps you saw it in the papers, though it was not put in as it should be. "Lately, George Wickham, Esquire, to Miss Lydia Bennet" and not a word about her parents or where she was from. They are gone to Newcastle, where he has joined a new regiment. Thank heavens he has *some* friends, poor Mr Wickham, though not as many as he deserves!

> *(That last comment is aimed at **MR DARCY**, who ignores it.)*

Do you plan to stay in the country long, Mr Bingley?

MR BINGLEY. A few weeks at least, and I hope to call on you again tomorrow morning, if I may.

MRS BENNET. Of course you may! And when you have killed all your own birds, you must come and shoot Mr Bennet's, too!

MR BINGLEY. You are all kindness, ma'am. Till tomorrow, then!

> (**ELIZABETH, JANE** *and* **MRS BENNET** *curtsy.*
> **MR DARCY** *gives a slight bow,* **MR BINGLEY**
> *bows, still smiling and moves upstage with*
> **MR DARCY** *while mime chatting.*)

MRS BENNET. What a fine young man he is! Such a pleasant manner! But why did he have to bring his friend?

> (**MRS BENNET** *and* **ELIZABETH** *cross and sit.*
> **JANE** *crosses and stands behind* **ELIZABETH**.
> *They freeze.*)

Transition To –

(Lights up only on **MR BINGLEY** *and* **MR DARCY** *right. They walk forward as* **MR BINGLEY** *states…)*

MR BINGLEY. You tell me now that she was in London all those months and you concealed it from me?

> *(***MR BINGLEY*** *is really displeased with his friend.)*

MR DARCY. Yes. I presumed to know your true feelings and Miss Bennet's, and I was wrong about both. I should not have interfered. It was wrong of me, and I apologise.

MR BINGLEY. You admit that you were in the wrong?

MR DARCY. Utterly and completely.

MR BINGLEY. Then I have your blessing?

MR DARCY. Do you need it?

MR BINGLEY. No, but I should like to have it all the same.

MR DARCY. Then go to it.

MR BINGLEY. Thank you. I shall.

> *(***MR BINGLEY*** *and* ***MR DARCY*** *shake hands before* ***MR BINGLEY*** *exits right. Lights go down on them and lights up left while* ***MR DARCY*** *exits right.* ***KITTY*** *runs on left, followed by* ***MARY***. ***MRS BENNET***, ***JANE*** *and* ***ELIZABETH*** *cross downstage.)*

KITTY. Jane! Mr Bingley's back! On his own this time!

MRS BENNET. Jane! Jane! Quick! Quick! Sit here where the light is flattering. Sit up straight. Chin up. Good. Don't move.

(JANE follows instructions. MARY comes and sits beside JANE.)

(Through gritted teeth to MARY.) What are you doing, you stupid girl?

(MR BINGLEY enters right and crosses centre. He bows. The BENNETs all curtsy.)

Mr Bingley, what a surprise! Will you walk into the little drawing-room?

(MR BINGLEY crosses left. JANE rises to greet him.)

Mary! You're wanted upstairs! Urgently!

(MRS BENNET ushers KITTY and ELIZABETH and they exit left. MARY takes her time about getting up, curtseying to MR BINGLEY and leaves the room exit left. Now MR BINGLEY and JANE are alone. MR BINGLEY moves closer to JANE, takes her hands and mimes speaking, we don't hear what MR BINGLEY is saying – but we do see Jane's delighted reaction. MR BINGLEY kisses Jane's hands. Pause. ELIZABETH walks in.)

ELIZABETH. Oh! I beg your pardon!

(MR BINGLEY and JANE move apart.)

MR BINGLEY. *(To JANE.)* I must speak to your father. Excuse me. *(MR BINGLEY exits upstage.)*

(JANE rushes to ELIZABETH and they hug.)

JANE. Oh, Lizzy! I am the happiest woman on earth! If only everyone could be as happy as I am! Do you know, he had no idea I was in London last spring! His sisters and Mr Darcy kept him in ignorance. He was in love with me all the time, Lizzy!

ELIZABETH. Of course he was. How could he not be?

>*(**MRS BENNET** comes bustling in left, and **MARY** and **KITTY** follow.)*

MRS BENNET. Mrs Bingley! How well that sounds! Well, he took his time about it, but he was worth waiting for.

KITTY. Jane, can Mary and me be bridesmaids?

>*(**MARY** shows her displeasure by nodding 'no'.)*

MRS BENNET. Of course you can, and Lizzy too! We'll see about all the wedding clothes directly!

>*(**MR BENNET** enters from upstage.)*

MR BENNET. Jane, I congratulate you. You will be a very happy woman.

>*(**JANE** goes and kisses **MR BENNET**.)*

You are very well-suited. You are each of you so complying, that nothing will ever be resolved on; so easy, that every servant will cheat you, and so generous, you will always exceed your income.

MRS BENNET. Exceed their income? Mr Bennet. Don't you know Bingley has *five thousand a year*?

JANE. I think I am the most fortunate creature that ever existed! Oh, Lizzy, I wish there was such another man for you!

ELIZABETH. Bingleys, I'm afraid, are in very short supply, but if I'm very lucky, I may meet another Mr Collins!

>*(**MR BENNET** and **JANE** exits upstage. **MRS BENNET** sits, **MARY** sits, **ELIZABETH** stands beside **MRS BENNET**. **KITTY** is looking out of window/offstage.)*

MRS BENNET. I hope they will settle for good at Netherfield; then we can see them every day. Lydia is much too far away.

(*Sound of four horse carriage arriving.*)

KITTY. Mama, the most enormous carriage is coming up the drive! With four horses!

MRS BENNET. Well! Whoever can that be?

KITTY. There's a lady getting out! She looks very grand!

(**ELIZABETH** *crosses to* **KITTY** *to look.*)

ELIZABETH. Oh, God! What is *she* doing here?

(**MAID** *comes in right.*)

MAID. If you please, ma'am, Lady Catherine de Bourgh.

(**MAID** *stands back to let* **LADY CATHERINE** *enter right.* **MRS BENNET**, **ELIZABETH**, **JANE** *and* **KITTY** *all curtsy.*)

MRS BENNET. (*All of a fluster.*) Lady Catherine! We are honoured! Of course, we know of your great kindness, do please sit down, oh I see you have!

(**LADY CATHERINE** *crosses left, having already sat down, stares round disparagingly.*)

LADY CATHERINE. I hope you are well, Miss Bennet.

ELIZABETH. I am, I thank you.

LADY CATHERINE. This lady I suppose is your mother.

ELIZABETH. Yes.

LADY CATHERINE. And these are two of your sisters?

ELIZABETH. They are.

MRS BENNET. My youngest is married, and my eldest is out walking with her fiancé, Mr Bingley.

LADY CATHERINE. Hm. You have a very small park here.

MRS BENNET. I dare say it's nothing to Rosings, my lady, but it's much larger than Sir William Lucas's!

LADY CATHERINE. Hmp. Miss Bennet, would you take a turn in the garden with me?

ELIZABETH. If you wish.

> (*Lights fade*. **MRS BENNET** *sits*, **JANE** *and* **KITTY** *stand and stay left and freeze*. **ELIZABETH** *and* **LADY CATHERINE** *cross downstage*.)

Transition To –

(Sound of birdsong and lights up on **ELIZABETH** *and* **LADY CATHERINE** *alone as if in a 'garden'.)*

LADY CATHERINE. Miss Bennet: a report of the most alarming nature has reached my ears: not only that your sister is to marry Mr Bingley, but that *you* have formed an attachment to my nephew!

ELIZABETH. What?

LADY CATHERINE. I know it is impossible, but I insist on being satisfied: has my nephew made you an offer of marriage or not?

ELIZABETH. Your ladyship has declared it to be impossible.

LADY CATHERINE. It ought to be so. Mr Darcy has long been engaged to *my daughter*. Now, what have you to say?

ELIZABETH. Only that if it is so, it's not likely that he'll make an offer to me.

LADY CATHERINE. Their engagement is of a peculiar kind; it was planned in their infancy. It was the favourite wish of his mother as well as mine. *(Her rage building.)* And now, to be thwarted by a young woman of inferior breeding!

ELIZABETH. Mr Darcy is a gentleman. I am a gentleman's daughter. In that respect we are equal.

LADY CATHERINE. But your mother! Your uncles and aunts! Your infamous youngest sister, with her patched-up marriage to a degenerate rogue and son of a steward! Are the shades of Pemberley to be thus corrupted?

(A pause before **ELIZABETH** *replies, quite calmly.)*

ELIZABETH. You can now have nothing further to say. You have insulted me in every possible way.

LADY CATHERINE. Will you promise me never to enter into an engagement with my nephew?

ELIZABETH. I will not.

LADY CATHERINE. *(Now very angry.)* Unfeeling, selfish girl! Very well! I now know how to act. I take no leave of you. I send no compliments to your mother. I am most seriously displeased.

> *(***LADY CATHERINE*** *stalks off right pushing* ***ELIZABETH*** *out of the way.* ***ELIZABETH*** *watches after* ***LADY CATHERINE*** *as she exits. Lights up left as* ***ELIZABETH*** *crosses to* ***MRS BENNET****.)*

MRS BENNET. Oh! Is she gone, then? Without saying goodbye? Well, these great folks have their little ways. I suppose she had nothing particular to say to you, Lizzy?

ELIZABETH. Nothing of consequence, Mamma.

> *(***KITTY*** *crosses to look out of window/offstage again.)*

KITTY. Mr Bingley's coming again! Oh, and he's brought his friend!

> *(***MRS BENNET*** *stands as* ***MAID*** *enters right.* ***MR BINGLEY*** *and* ***MR DARCY*** *enter right.)*

MAID. Mr Bingley and Mr Darcy, ma'am.

> *(***MAID*** *curtsies and exits right.* ***MRS BENNET***, ***JANE***, ***ELIZABETH*** *and* ***KITTY*** *all curtsy and* ***MR DARCY*** *and* ***MR BINGLEY*** *bow.*

This meeting is awkward for **MR DARCY** *and* **ELIZABETH**. *A simple pleasure for* **MR BINGLEY** *and* **JANE**.)

MR BINGLEY. It is a fine day: should we perhaps all walk towards Meryton?

(**MRS BENNET** *and* **KITTY** *exit left.* **MR BINGLEY** *offers his arm to* **JANE**. **MR DARCY** *offers his arm for* **ELIZABETH**. *They walk upstage. Lights down, chairs off.)*

Transition To –

(Sound of birdsong as lights fade up. **ELIZABETH** *and* **MR DARCY** *walk downstage, friendly but unsure.* **JANE** *and* **MR BINGLEY** *following, chatting and smiling.)*

MR DARCY. *(While walking downstage.)* I apologise for my absence latterly. I had some matters to deal with.

ELIZABETH. Mr Darcy, before we go any further I must thank you for your great kindness towards my poor sister.

MR DARCY. You were not supposed to be informed. I did not think Mrs Gardiner was so little to be trusted.

ELIZABETH. You mustn't blame my aunt. Lydia let it all out by accident.

> *(**JANE** and **BINGLEY** have walked on and exit to leave **ELIZABETH** and **MR DARCY** alone.)*

MR DARCY. Well – if you must thank me, let it be for yourself alone. Your family owe me nothing. Much as I respect them, I thought only of you.

ELIZABETH. *(Softly.)* Oh.

MR DARCY. You are too generous to trifle with me. If your feelings are still what they were last April, tell me at once. My affections are unchanged, but one word from you will silence me for ever.

ELIZABETH. Oh...my feelings are – I am ashamed to remember what they were then. My feelings are very different. In fact, they are quite the opposite!

MR DARCY. Truly?

ELIZABETH. Truly.

MR DARCY. Then –

ELIZABETH. Yes. I will marry you.

*(**MR DARCY** takes **ELIZABETH**'s hand and kisses it.)*

MR DARCY. Lady Catherine told me of your meeting with her. It taught me to hope. I knew that if you had decided absolutely against me, you would have told her.

ELIZABETH. Yes – having abused you to your face.

MR DARCY. I deserved everything you said to me back then. I have been a selfish being all my life. And such I might still have been, but for you, dearest, loveliest Elizabeth!

(Lights fade on both of them centre with love theme music. They kiss tentatively. **MR DARCY** whispers in Elizabeth's ear and exits upstage to go to talk to **MR BENNET**. **ELIZABETH** is so happy Pause before **MRS BENNET** enters left.)*

MRS BENNET. Lizzy, I'm sorry you had to have that disagreeable man all to yourself! And now he's gone to talk to Mr Bennet, the good Lord knows why! – I wish he would go away and not bother us again!

*(**MR BENNET** enters from upstage. He dismisses **MRS BENNET** who exits left.)*

MR BENNET. Lizzy. A word.

*(**MR BENNET** and **ELIZABETH** are alone.)*

What are you doing? Are you out of your senses, accepting this man? Have you not always hated him? He is rich, to be sure. But can he make you happy?

---

* A licence to produce *Pride and Prejudice* does not include a performance licence for any third-party or copyrighted recordings. Licensees should create their own

ELIZABETH. Have you any other objections, besides my supposed dislike of him?

MR BENNET. None at all.

ELIZABETH. Then, I do like him. I do. I love him. You don't know what he really is.

MR BENNET. Lizzy, I have already given him my consent. He is the kind of man one does not refuse. But I beg you to reconsider. A marriage *(Looking offstage after* **MRS BENNET.***)* is a miserable state of things when one partner cannot truly respect the other.

ELIZABETH. I do, I do respect him. It was he who brought about Lydia's marriage, and paid for everything, even though Mr Wickham had betrayed him in every way. He did it for me. He is truly the best of men. He has no unseemly pride.

MR BENNET. Well, my dear, if this be the case, he deserves you. I could not have parted with you to anyone less worthy. Off you go now. If any young men come for Mary or Kitty, send them in, for I am quite at leisure.

*(***MRS BENNET** *comes on left, in raptures.)*

MRS BENNET. Good gracious! Lord bless me! Mr Darcy! Who'd have thought it? Oh, my sweetest Lizzy! *(She hugs* **ELIZABETH.***)* How rich and grand you will be! Ten thousand a year! Three daughters married! Oh Lord! What will become of me? I shall go distracted! Mr Bennet! Mr Bennet! *(She exits upstage.)*

(Lights up onstage, dance music starts. **ELIZABETH** *is briefly alone onstage looking so happy. Immediately* **MRS BENNET** *exits,* **JANE***,* **KITTY** *and* **MARY** *enter to hug*

---

* A licence to produce *Pride and Prejudice* does not include a performance licence for any third-party or copyrighted recordings. Licensees should create their own

ELIZABETH *centre as if in celebration of her marriage to* **MR DARCY**. **LYDIA** *and* **MR WICKHAM** *enter with* **LYDIA** *giving* **ELIZABETH** *a hug.* **MR WICKHAM** *stands aside.* **BINGLEY** *and* **MR DARCY** *enter and take* **JANE** *and* **ELIZABETH** *by the hand and, with* **LYDIA** *and* **MR WICKHAM**, *into a dance. Everyone else enters and, [except for* **LADY CATHERINE** *who is not pleased with the union], clap along to the music. After dance lights can fade to come back up for the curtain call.)*

The End

CHARACTERS AND COSTUMES

All Bennet sisters in light pastel colours. Each sister wears one dress each (under bust Georgian-style dress) each in a different colour to ensure the audience knows who is who! Capes/coats, evening gloves and an overdress for Netherfield Ball. Shoes and tights.

ELIZABETH BENNET – A cape which can easily be taken off and on as she does not have time to change. Also, possibly a pinafore to go over costume which is muddy along the bottom which can easily be put on with her cape. Also, muddy shoes.

MARY BENNET – More prudish dress with possibly a higher neck.

LYDIA – Dress with a round neck preferred.

MR BENNET – Long trousers/breaches, white shirt, plain waistcoat, jacket, necktie, boots or shoes. For Netherfield Ball, different waistcoat and jacket.

MRS BENNET – One dress (waisted), could be a blouse and long skirt, shoes and tights. Cape/Coat. Overdress for Netherfield Ball.

MR FITZWILLIAM DARCY – Breaches, boots, socks, white shirts (x2, one wet for Act Two scene and one dry), embroidered waistcoat, necktie and jacket.

GEORGIANA DARCY – Similar dress to Bennet sisters, pastel colour, cape/coat (borrow one of the Bennet capes), shoes and tights.

MR CHARLES BINGLEY – Similar to Mr Darcy, breaches, boots, socks, white shirt, waistcoat, necktie, jacket.

MISS CAROLINE BINGLEY – Darker richer-coloured dress, headdress feathers, evening gloves, shoes and tights.

MRS HURST – Darker richer-coloured dress, sparkly headress, evening gloves, shoes and tights.

SIR WILLIAM LUCAS – Similar to Mr Bennet, long trousers/breaches, white shirt, plain waistcoat, jacket, necktie, boots or shoes.

CHARLOTTE LUCAS – Similar to Bennet girls, plain pastel-coloured dress, evening gloves, over pinafore dress for Netherfield Ball, shoes and tights.

MR COLLINS – Clergy outfit, black breaches, white shirt, necktie, high black waistcoat, black jacket, black shoes and black long socks.

LADY CATHERINE DE BOURGH – Dark velvet outfit, could be skirt, jacket and blouse or dress (with jacket), impressive headdress/hat to match, shoes and tights.

LADY ANNE DE BOURGH – Dark brown/black outfit, prefer dress, headdress with small veil, shoes and tights.

GEORGE WICKHAM – Period red military uniform with all the trimmings! Will be taking jacket off so require shirt and necktie underneath.

DENNY – Will not be taking jacket off so no need for shirt underneath.

MR GARDINER – Similar to Mr Bennet, breeches/trousers, white shirt, necktie, plain waistcoat, jacket, boots/shoes and socks.

MRS GARDINER – Similar to Mrs Bennet, dress or jacket and skirt, lacey blouse, shoes and tights, cape/coat (could borrow from one of the Bennet girls).

MRS REYNOLDS – Working class dress, dark/grey colour, could be skirt and blouse, sturdy shoes and tights. Not a maid outfit, no apron or hat.

HANNAH (OR HARRY) – Working class outfit in dull colours. Trousers/breeches, shirt, necktie, waistcoat, shoes and black socks. Or skirt and blouse depending on gender.

MAID – Georgian maid black dress, white full-length apron and white mop cap.

BUTLER – Typical butler, breaches, long socks, shoes, waistcoat, white shirt, necktie, black jacket. Part of the action with no lines and is required to serve, move chairs and assist with scene changes.

Plus any **EXTRAS/DANCERS** for ball scenes as required.

SIR WILLIAM/MR GARDINER – could be similar outfits base costumes with a change of jacket.

DENNY – dance partner in Act One – requires a different jacket and possibly breeches but base costumes can be the same for military uniform. Likely to also be Harry, servant, no jacket, different waistcoat but shirt and breeches can be same as dance partner.

MR COLLINS – dance partner in Act One – requires a different waistcoat and jacket, rest can be the same.

MRS HURST/MRS GARDINER – Mrs Hurst appears in Act One and Mrs Gardiner appears in Act Two. Require two different dresses/ costumes.

LADY ANNE/GEORGIANA – two different dresses!

HAIR – will try to reduce number of wigs by the girls styling own hair up in the typical Georgian style. Except Lady Catherine who is most likely going to need a very grand wig! Men's hair will keep as natural but hope they will grow their own sideburns!

Quick Changes:

Act One, Scene Seven – Elizabeth – muddy coat, overdress and shoes.

Act One, Scene Thirteen – Charlotte, Mr and Mrs Bennet, Lizzy, Jane, Kitty, Lydia and Mary – for Netherfield Ball, overdresses and gloves.

Act One, Scene Fourteen – Mrs Bennet, Elizabeth, Kitty, Jane, Lydia and Mary, out of overdresses, gloves from ball to go back home to Longbourn.

Act Two, Scene Six – Mr Darcy from wet shirt scene to dry shirt, necktie and jacket.

PROPERTY AND FURNITURE LIST

Personal props:
Mrs Bennet – lace hankie
Mary – round reading glasses and small book
Mr Bennet – half reading glasses
Lady Catherine – walking stick

ACT ONE		
Page/Scene	**Who/Where**	**What**
Pre-set	On rostra	Chaise and one chair.
		Desk/small table with writing materials on top. Or writing slope.
	Offstage	3 Chairs for use during various scenes.
	Offstage	1 piano and stool, sheet music on piano.
Scene Three	Mr Bennet	Book, bring on with him.
Scene Five	On piano for Mary	Sheet music.
Scene Six	Maid	Letter/note open from Netherfield for Jane.
Scene Seven	Mr Darcy	Gun – large musket type.
Scene Eight	Jane	Sheet, pillow and shawl as if in bed on the chaise.
Scene Ten	Elizabeth	Book, pre-set.
Scene Ten	Mrs Hurst	Playing cards.
Scene Ten	Mr Darcy	Desk and chair or writing slope, paper and quill on a chair.
	Mr Bennet	Letter open from Mr Collins.
Scene Twelve	Elizabeth	Comb.
Scene Twelve	Mrs Bennet	Invitation to Netherfield Ball.
Scene Twelve	Maid brings on basket for Lydia, Kitty, Jane and Elizabeth	Basket with long pieces of ribbon, lengths of lace, long pieces of material. They need to be long enough bits to wave around! They help themselves.

Scene Thirteen	Mary	Sheet music taken onstage for use during scene.
Scene Fourteen	Jane	Open letter from Miss Bingley.
	Mary	Book.
	Elizabeth	Book.
	Lydia and Kitty	Bonnet and ribbons.
	Mrs Bennet	Sewing.
Scene Fifteen	Charlotte	Desk with writing materials or writing slope, paper and quill.
Scene Fifteen	Elizabeth	Travel bag and cape for maid to bring on.
Scene Seventeen	Elizabeth	Sheet music on piano.
Scene Eighteen	Maid	Open letter from Jane.
	Elizabeth	Sheet music on piano.
Scene Twenty One	Elizabeth	Desk with writing materials or writing slope, paper and quill.
ACT TWO		
Scene One	Mr Darcy	Desk or writing slope/box, paper and quill. Candle and holder. Sealed Letter.
Scene One	Charlotte	Shopping basket with items inside. None are taken out or used.
Scene Two	Elizabeth	Travel bag and cape. Already set onstage.
Scene Three	Lydia	Bonnet and some ribbon.
	Mary	Book.
	Mrs Bennet	Sewing.
	Jane	Sewing.
Scene Three	Lydia	Travel bag/case (different to Elizabeths) and cape.
Scene Four	Maid	Capes for Elizabeth and Mrs Gardiner.
Scene Five	Hannah	Two folded sheets to carry on.
Scene Six	Hannah	Tray and three half full port glasses.
Scene Seven	Elizabeth	Sheet music on piano.

Scene Eight	Hannah	Sealed letter from Jane for Elizabeth.
Scene Eleven	Maid	Smelling salts bottle for Mrs Bennet.
Scene Nine	Mr Collins	Small bible.
Scene Ten	Wickham	Desk with writing materials or writing slope, small notebook, quill, empty beer bottle.
Scene Eleven	Maid	Sealed letter from Mr Bennet.
Scene Eleven	Maid	Tray with one tea cup and saucer for Mr Bennet.
Scene Thirteen	Kitty	Sealed letter from Mr Gardiner.
Scene Thirteen	Maid	Sealed letter from village friend.

Properties have been kept to a minimum but more could be added. There are a lot of letters!

LIGHTING – Lighting was used to identify different areas and locations. Generally lighting is mentioned within the script. The lighting can be as complicated or as easy as required.

Proposed set enables different locations within the one set.

MUSIC AND SOUND EFFECTS LIST

The music listed below is suggested music, a licence to produce *Pride and Prejudice* does not include a performance licence for any third-party or copyrighted music. Licensees should create an original composition or use music in the public domain. For further information, please see the Music and Third-Party Materials Use Note on page iii

ACT ONE		
Scene	**When/details**	**What**
Scene One	Opening	Joseph Haydn, Piano Sonata no 53 in E Minor, Hob XV1:34: III Vivace. Also used throughout as link music.
Scene Two	Scene change	Piano music taken from Haydn sonata in E-Flat major, Hob XV:52: 1 Allegro.
Scene Two	Country Dance music at beg of scene.	Assembly Room dance music Three Around Three (Polka)/Speed the Plough. The English Country Dance Band.
Scene Five	Piano played by Mary into scene Concerto	Mary's bad playing at the start of scene. Wolfgang Mozart, Minuet in D Major, K.355 played by Wanda Landowska.
Scene Five	Piano played by Mary for the dance – jig, Speaking throughout the dance!	Harpsichord piano for Mary, dance music. Number: 7 – Trip to Dillington from Ignatius Sancho: 12 Country Dances for the year 1779 (Harpsichord).
Scene Six	Scene change, dance music as above.	Same as above.
Scene Six	**Thunder, lightning, rain**	n/a
Scene Seven	**Birdsong/countryside**	n/a
Scene Eight	Link music	Opening piano music from: Joseph Haydn, Piano Sonata no 53 in E Minor, Hob XV1:34: III Vivace.

Scene Nine	Link music.	Same again.
Scene Ten	Link music.	Same again.
Scene Eleven	**Birdsong/countryside**	n/a
Scene Twelve	Scene change – lively music for sisters to get ready for Ball fade into...	Mozart, Sonata No. 16 C Major (Sonata Facile, KV545 (1788).
Scene Thirteen	Background music of ball for scene change and welcome guests.	Piano music taken from Haydn sonata in E-Flat major, Hob XV:52: 1 Allegro.
Scene Thirteen	Stately dance music two minutes. Mr Darcy and Elizabeth chat throughout!	Netherfield Ball dance The English Dance Master: Vol 1: The Beggar Boy, John Playford, Baltimore Consort.
Scene Thirteen	Mary playing a bad/ boring piece of music.	Same piece as Scene Five Mozart Minuet in D Major, K355 but on a piano.
Scene Thirteen	Mrs Hurst playing a lovely piece of music, plays out the scene.	Mozart Piano sonata no 13 in B flat, K333: 1. Allegro.
Scene Fourteen	Half-way down page, Time passing, Music to accompany movement.	Joseph Haydn, Piano Sonata no 53 in E Minor, Hob XV1:34: III Vivace.
Scene Seventeen	Scene change music for Lady C.	Rachmaninov: 10 Preludes, Op.23: No 5 in G Minor.
Scene Twenty	Elizabeth plays piano. She stops playing and then plays same piece of music again which goes into playing the scene out.	Clementi Sonatina No 1 in C Major, Op 36:1 Allegro for piano Elizabeth playing music at Roslings.
Scene Twenty One	End of Act music after Mr Darcy has gone off.	Haydn keyboard sonata in E-Flat major, Hob XV:52: 1 Allegro. Opening bars of music.
ACT TWO		
Scene	**When/details**	**What**
Scene One	Opening Act Two – same as end of Act Two.	Same as end of Act One. Haydn keyboard sonata in E-Flat major, Hob XV:52: 1 Allegro. Opening bars of music.

Scene One	**Owl hooting as lights fade, pause then into early morning birdsong chorus.**	n/a
Scene Four	**Birdsong/countryside.**	n/a
Scene Five	**Birdsong.**	n/a
Scene Seven	Elizabeth playing piano – coming to the end of a piece of music.	Clementi Sonatina No 1 in C Major, Op 36:1 Allegro for Elizabeth playing piano at Pemberley.
Scene Seven	Georgiana playing piano – pauses when Mr Wickham is mentioned. Continues to end of scene.	Passacaglia/Handel instrumental version piano played by Santiago Melo Our Love theme!
Scene Twenty One	Music scene change dramatic after "Mr Darcy!"	Haydn Keyboard sonata in E-Flat major, Hob XV:52: 1 Allegro. Opening bars for music. Same as end of Act One piece of music.
Scene Thirteen	**4 horse carriage arriving**	n/a
Scene Thirteen	**Birdsong/countryside.**	n/a
Scene Thirteen	Background love music for Elizabeth and Mr Darcy's kiss.	Again bit of... Passacaglia/ Handel instrumental version piano played by Santiago Melo. Love theme!
Scene Thirteen	After Elizabeth says last line as a celebration.	Celebration music. Same as scene two dance music. Three Around Three (Polka)/Speed the Plough. The English Country Dance Band. Some of the cast go into a quick celebration dance.
End of Act Two	Curtain call. Same as beginning of Act One.	Joseph Haydn, Piano Sonata no 53 in E Minor, Hob XV1:34: III Vivace.